How to have a beautiful life now
Happy

CHRISTIAN FEEGER

Copyright © Christian Feeger

All rights reserved.

No part of this publication may be reproduced, stored in a retrieval system, or transmitted in any form or by any means, electronic, mechanical, photocopying, recording or otherwise, without the prior written permission of the author.

First published in 2012 by Return to Work, Australia
Printed and bound by Lightning Source Printers

ISBN 9780987194800

Cover design by Holly Webber
Typesetting by Mairi Feeger

www.happy.fm

Starting with nothing more than a vision in a quiet café one windy spring, this book grew. Along the way these people helped me make it happen, and I am grateful to each one. People like: Pete Walsh for listening so much… Helen Behrens for encouraging me very early on… my dear Aunt Anschen Stoertzer for her incredible positivity… my sister, Eva Renn, and brother, Alex Feeger, for their ongoing support… serene Jo Richardson for her well-timed insights… Astrid Ølgaard Christensen for brainstorming near the beginning... dear Michelle Morgenstern for her enduring reassurance…. Phillipa and Michael Power for presuming it would happen… observant Matt Bain for discerning beauty comes in either little or big "B"... and my dear wife, Ruth, who in believing beyond reason has listened, loved, and endured so much to support her daring dreamer. Thank you.

Foreword

Keats said *"A thing of beauty is a joy forever."*

The quest for beauty has consumed generations and is the driving force behind multimillion-dollar corporations.

Yet so little attention is given to nurturing the beauty that lasts forever and this is why you should read this book.

I can give you at least three reasons to do so:

We all have need of an encouraging friend and that's certainly what you will get if you keep reading. I have enjoyed Christians' friendship for more than thirty years and have often been the recipient of his encouragement through affirmation and validation. Now you can also escape from the internal and external voices of criticism and set your attention on nurturing your beautiful self and in turn a beautiful life.

Our relationships need to be emancipated from the chains of family history, the impact of current circumstances and our fractured sense of self. Instead of playing out well-worn patterns of behaviour, Christian presents us with tools to create sustaining relationships, characterised by appreciation, honesty, and encouragement. In overcoming the adversities and challenges of his own life, Christian chooses to live what he speaks. I can vouch for his enduring, loving marriage, family, and friendships.

The power of lives lived in beautiful integrity can change a world steeped in the ugliness of selfishness, self-recrimination, loneliness and despair. Christian reminds us of how to live in the mindfulness of the moment. Taking time to appreciate the beauty around you and responding to it. In his own life Christian is very deliberate in his quest to act on these principles. By creating our own unique responses we have an opportunity to plant beauty in the world around us. These responses, even the tiniest, will spread the mark of true beauty into a world that is impoverished by its lack.

So take this opportunity for a friend to help you to reflect on what drives your inner life and relationships. Take the time to practice making choices that create beauty and watch it blossom and grow into a beautiful life and a beautiful world.

Ann Fraser
Senior Social Worker
Grief Counseling and Family Therapy

Contents

FOREWORD *by Ann Fraser*		i
1	*Wanted: True Beauty*	3
2	*Awareness Reflection Action*	20
3	*Revealing The Seven Strengths*	43
4	*Beautiful Meaning*	66
5	*Releasing Your Happiness*	91
6	*Building a Beautiful Life*	109
7	*Living Beautifully*	130
8	*Conquering Emotional Chaos*	154
9	*Working Beautifully*	177
10	*Growing Relationships*	197
Appendix		215
Suggested Reading		219
Index		222

Chapter 1

Wanted: True Beauty

"Let the beauty we love be what we do"

Rumi

More Than Looking Good

Before you go any further, I want to encourage you to loosen up, let go, and be yourself. Looking good is fine. But there are other features to living a beautiful life. So let's explore how to make your *life* more beautiful.

First off, I'm *not* going to advise you how to have a firmer, flatter tummy in two weeks. Or to only obey "this rule." Fashion tips too, have been deliberately excluded from this manual. Just like your skin-cleansing regime, they are all off the agenda. In fact, I can personally guarantee your physical beauty routine will be kept free from tampering.

Not that your physical appearance is unimportant. All forms of beauty are a delight, aren't they? It's just with so many books out there on looks already, don't you think it's time we started widening our view? We need to discover what we've been missing.

> *"It takes more than just a good looking body. You've got to have the heart and soul to go with it."*
>
> From The Discourses of Epictetus

This book is about a grander view of beauty. Beauty that gives you a zest for living and a profound sense of happiness.

By helping to unwrap the gift of your own beauty, I want to encourage you to understand more about who you are and how you can do *"you"* well.

Too often, beauty feels like something outside of us, about others, or something we still need to buy. But the view in this book is different. Think of it as beauty with a capital *"B."* Physical appearance is just one small part.

So, if you've ever yearned to be more, keep reading. There's no need to become angry, deny attractiveness, or get rebellious. True beauty is liberating as it is.

If you have spent your life living with self-doubts, this view will comfort and inspire you. Even in the toughest situations, it will help you in expressing the best of yourself. Instead of taking mirror measurements of your self-worth, I want you to discover more that is beautiful about *you*. By exploring what matters most to you and discovering new strengths, I want you to be empowered.

On the way, I'll tell you a bit about myself. So you get a sense of my quest.

So, what are we talking about? What is beauty after all?

Many people believe beauty is perfectly expressed in visual appeal. Say, in the look of an attractive woman. Then again, beauty is also used as a catchall term. A word to describe the best of everything.

We know beauty gives our senses satisfaction. So, *"whatever gladdens mind or spirit"* might be a worthwhile definition. When we experience beauty, something happens. It's as if we connect with quality, *personally*. Still, pinning it down is hard, isn't it? By nature, beauty refuses to be plainly described or measured. This gives thinkers plenty to chew over.

Philosophers have gone to great lengths trying to measure it using reason. But beauty's subtlety and delicacy keep preventing it from being absolutely classified. To date, nobody has succeeded in putting it into a box, marked *"we know."* Instead, people keep disagreeing about precisely *what* beauty is. Worse, what is captivating to one might be plain boring to another. For instance, picture yourself amidst a field of flowers, on a warm, sunny day. Breathing deeply, you inhale their sweet, subtle perfume. Gradually, a soothing calm is beginning to spread over you, putting you at ease.

You might find this a pleasant enough image. After all, flowers are a familiar symbol of beauty. Yet, their loveliness isn't universally appreciated. Some see them as signs of sickness, forewarning the coming of yet more hay fever. For them this inspiring display only conjures dismay. Likewise, when it comes to the latest fashion creations, style critics begin bickering about designer magic or otherwise, long before the stores are stocked.

Turning to the media, we seek expert information to give us an opinion about the latest sensation. Knowing what we like is all right, but are we *right*? Collectively, our hesitancy keeps us hunting for opinions. Wanting to know what's in, what's out, what is, and what's not. Sad to say, it seems we don't trust ourselves. Fortunately, if nothing else, we all agree on this one point: to be beautiful something must be profoundly pleasing. When it is, it wins our admiration and inspires us to share the pleasure with the world.

Uniting the World

Instead of division, there is something unifying about true beauty. It's like powerful glue. But instead of forcibly holding us, it joins us together without pressure. Beauty satisfies because it is so captivating. Even if our own version is unique, we still share a knowing. To be touched by beauty is something everybody understands.

No matter what we like, we can all discern it to varying degrees. It is simply remarkable. Just think, despite all of humanity's differences, we share this common connection. Regardless of race, creed, or culture, we can see beauty crossing all boundaries.

Every person in every society around the world values what beauty gives. Over the ages, it keeps on being a uniting strength. Whether enjoying music, experiencing art, or delighting in any number of qualities, our appreciation keeps bringing us together. Just as actions of beauty build trust, all of us are capable of putting value into our efforts. Living as we mean to, we can choose to grace our days with something strong.

Doing so nurtures understanding too. The more we live in the light of beauty, the more we can recognize ugly intentions and behavior.

Yet, it is also true that there is much dividing us. Consider how many people are spending today in ugliness. Some, bent on destroying the lives of others, are wreaking havoc through their decisions. Could they grasp that beauty was also in their hands?

Before people begin choosing beauty, I believe they need to know it and own it for themselves. The more they understand beauty, the less likely they are to be consumed by ugliness and chaos. In a world where things keep changing constantly, sometimes instantaneously, there is also room for steadiness and assurance.

You and I live in worlds apart where our daily experiences never meet. But because we welcome beauty's compelling power, we share a common understanding. It goes beyond distance and difference so that together, we share what matters.

Beauty Worth Believing In

Take a look in the mirror, and there you are. Or is there more? What you see is your outward appearance, with all of your inherited physical features and flaws. But that's just your wrapping, isn't it?

Your *spirit*, soul, or sense of self barely gets a thought. Yet isn't that what makes you *you*?

> *"Many of the things you can count, don't count. Many of the things you can't count, really count."*
>
> Albert Einstein

According to the advertisers, your highest quest is craving flawless, youthful skin, a new face, and modellesque perfection. It is beauty reduced to skin deep looks. So if you perceive precious little beauty gazing critically into the mirror, it's more than deflating. It's rejection. We can never be okay that way.

Having personal beauty so distorted is taking its toll. So much so, we're letting go of something vital. We're forgetting the value of our dignity.

You may not be thinking about it but deep down you know that becoming more beautiful begins in your *mind*. There, your power to choose has the capacity to energize you. Your mind has the ability to make beautiful things happen. It can even convey that feeling to everyone you meet.

So, if the source of your beauty is in your spirit, you can decide how to show it. The wisest of people show the beauty of their spirit, rather than merely the beauty of their form.

Becoming more beautiful can be about agreeing to greater *honesty* with yourself. Accepting what you have and what you do not have allows you to relax in your self. In turn, being candid about your nature will endear you to others. This is not surprising as people of quality admire *honesty*.

For some, getting fitter is the thing that comes to mind when they think about "beauty." Deciding to improve our health might be the way to find how much more beautiful life can be. Having energy and feeling a sense of control over our physical selves can certainly be profoundly satisfying.

Others choose to pour their qualities into their career path. Daring to be who they always dreamed they could be. Reaching out and taking up a challenge can mean everything if we are inspired to pursue a goal.

Then there are those who throw their all into charity work. Believing that *giving* is one of the greatest ways to live life well they find beauty in being able to help. Not only do they benefit others, their altruism also boosts their sense of well-being and psychological resilience.

To some extent, each of these actions is about making the world a better place. Likewise, when you develop your noble passions, you have the potential to make great things happen.

You might be thinking all of this is fine. But how does this relate to me, considering everything I've got going on in my life? The answer, I believe, is that you and I have the power to create our own version of beauty. It's a force that doesn't need to wait for anything, much less the ideal time.

The deep truths of discovering your beauty cannot simply be boxed up into a cosmetic kit. Choosing to live your life more beautifully is much more about what you consider and how you live. When it comes to being beautiful, looks are less significant than we think. Beauty turns out to be a *doing* word.

If you happen to be blessed with perfect skin, a gorgeous body, and a perfectly proportioned face, of course that's fantastic. But that doesn't necessarily mean you're living a beautiful life right now.

We all love beauty, and its outward appearance is the cause of constant, almost exhausting, worship. But delightful as it is, pretty packaging won't satisfy. We know because even with it we keep on seeking greater *satisfaction*. This, of course, is precisely what we need. Feeling *fulfillment* is the only thing that will take us further. As it does, we can discover more beauty than good looks alone could possibly offer.

This then is a journey into the heart of beauty according to how *you* translate it. Here, your meaning can unleash loveliness or hold it back. By shaping your awareness and creativity, belief will determine everything.

This is why those living a haphazard or disconnected life end up feeling so much dissatisfaction. Meeting thousands of people over the years professionally and personally, I am certain that the richer your life is with personal meaning, the more beautiful you can expect it to be.

Beginning a Revolution

On the surface, this simple shift in awareness seems nothing dramatic. There is no swearing of allegiance or financial commitment. No rigorous training is imposed by anyone. Nor is there any bearded guru to obey or strict formula to follow.

Living beautifully is your choice. Dedicating your life to beauty is in your hands. You may be consciously doing so already. Or maybe, you somehow feel your life needs changing. By embracing life with open arms, this is the time for discovering the joys you've been missing.

Wherever you are, the key to unlocking your own capacities is in *you*. Using whatever form of beauty you choose is at the core of your influence. The more you apply it, the more it will keep nourishing your actions and ideas.

> **"The most courageous act is still to think for yourself. Aloud."**
>
> Coco Chanel

Right now, there are people around you on their own personal journey. Like you, they are expressing beauty too. Whether they fully grasp their influence or not, it's exciting to see what they're doing.

There are a select few who, like you, are already *deliberately* using their power to appreciate and create. You, knowing as much as you do, already have a connection with them. Like you, they seek to live a more fulfilling life.

You may be a world and a lifetime of experiences away, but whether they're across the county, country, or on other side of the world, your shared understanding unites you. Hand in hand, you share the same guiding principles.

Just as you are now, no matter where you live, your growing understanding can unleash extraordinary beauty. By expressing it, you can enrich every one of your relationships. Realizing this underscores your importance.

Although disarmingly simple, this is a revolution of astonishing power. By bringing down personal walls, it can renew hope and forge new friendships. Producing beauty lets you tap into a tremendous healing force. Using its essence, you generate goodwill, both personally and publicly.

Relating through the common bond of beauty, you join others in speaking a language of influence. Overcoming your personal limitations, it helps you replace disunity with something we all crave: acceptance.

Domination, division, and selfish desires become increasingly meaningless in its light. Desperate grasping looks sad and ugly. With beauty's balancing sway, money starts assuming its rightful place: not propping up inadequacy but serving as a useful tool. Relationships firmly take center stage.

Graciousness and mutual respect take priority over politeness and ceremony. Through the purpose and potency of beauty, we have a reason for living well. With it, together we can bring out the best in our family, our community, and ourselves.

Knowing You Are Okay

Nearly everyone struggles with self-confidence at some point. Even the most outspoken and outwardly confident privately know the feeling of insecurity. Their hidden anxiety is that others will find out, seeing them for what they are. Game over.

> *"The good life is inspired by love and guided by knowledge."*
> Bertrand Russell

Our inferiority feeds all sorts of destructive behavior, doesn't it? Putting others down so we can feel up or sniping about weaknesses are symptoms of our struggles within. Inferiority plays its cards through distrusting, deceiving, and crippling our self-confidence.

Growing up in a home where criticism and sarcasm were the default setting, I, like so many, know personally how self-doubt touches us at every level.

Even in loving one another, we struggle with self-acceptance. Notice how many love songs say things like *"Don't leave me, I'm nothing without you"* as if the person they adore is the only reason to live. This is more than feeling intense passion. The celebration of empty desperateness is a revealing statement in itself. When longing for someone switches to feeling worthless without them, it's a declaration of self-doubt.

Unless a partner is driven by power, wouldn't they want their adoring lover to feel good about themselves too? Except, of course, if they're feeling inadequate too. In that case, matching their low confidence reassures them there's no need to grow.

Compare that with a deep and satisfying love. When someone loves you like that, they want you to feel *fulfilled*. They delight in seeing you happy being yourself: not just a co-star in a dependency partnership but a person to love with admiration and respect.

When the love-smitten aura starts subsiding, and it does, it's clear the perfect partner only lives in our imagination. No matter how lovely they are, or how marvelous we see ourselves as being, partners are genuinely human. Being human qualifies us all to be flawed and sometimes even painfully stupid. Twenty-nine years into married life, Ruth and I have passed the aura stage. But we're happy to say love gets grander the further we go. How? I guess knowing she loves me despite my weaknesses makes me appreciate her all the more.

Fortunately, we each have the capacity to also be wonderful, even strangely fascinating, to each other. Sharing your ability to be both is at the core of you and I being our beautiful selves.

To share it, you need to let your trust in *you* come through. Having barriers to overcome that restrict our self-belief is normal. Belief barriers like *"I'm too fat,"* *"too thin,"* *"too plain,"* or *"too something"* are keeping us down. The fact that they tend to focus on body acceptance reflects the spirit of the times. But you are infinitely more than your body.

Breaking through these entrenched beliefs requires action. Doing something worthwhile gives you at least a glimpse that you are much more, that you can do things and have potential. This, I believe, is crucial because doing more requires both *belief* and *action*. One without the other won't work.

Simply being told you're beautiful simply isn't enough. Quickly, you will dismiss such talk as fake flattery or, at best, well intentioned but lacking in fact. Having spent a lifetime being told what's wrong with us, feeling okay about ourselves is going to take some work.

Seeing better in yourself requires doing things that boost your self-respect. Each time you do, you will be building a better sense of identity. Fortunately, you only need a bit of awareness and determination to begin it. No other qualifications are necessary.

When it comes to becoming more beautiful, I've noticed a consistent pattern. Looks and brains are lovely things. But what really counts is *attitude*.

Lacking stunning looks isn't the problem we've been led to believe it is. The problem is feeling bad about being who we are. This feeling ruins everything.

Imagine one day the potential existed to make you look perfectly attractive in appearance. From follicle to cuticle, your physique is made immaculate, according to one perfected style.

Now assume everyone else also has access to this amazing technology. Then what? Would you believe you had finally become the beauty you longed to be? Or, looking identical to everyone else, would you feel something was wrong? Attractive beyond words, perhaps. But what's lacking would be your *uniqueness*.

There is something about your essence that really makes beauty shine.

Okay, I know this is all so deeply ingrained it's hard to untangle. Much of our feelings about beauty are bound up by self-sabotaging, tending to cancel us out.

By believing that beauty is either bought or only belongs to the lucky, it's easy to feel excluded. Thanks to the fantasies of marketing, the Joneses we're supposedly keeping up with are now looking increasingly rich and exaggerated. Thanks to the out of control machine of promotion, that's short-circuiting our sense of balance.

The process is harnessing and exploiting our innate desire to compare ourselves; a habit that's hard to ignore. That's why I believe it's high time we claimed back our reality minus ad breaks. It's time to give the phony image of family perfection the heave ho.

Real people, you in fact, live a life full of experience, grit, and self-expression. Pretending to give us greater expressiveness, advertisers, meanwhile, work hard to link product to passion. So we can buy our identity in a wide range of features and colors. Though wouldn't you know it? They just ran out of them in our size.

Feeling okay about ourselves right now relies on us taking control of how we operate. Thinking about what matters most to us personally is paramount.

Otherwise, forfeiting our personal beauty means stomaching the lie that all we can do is buy so the con can keep continuing. Believing that means purchasing *Brand X* will be the only way to prove we're okay.

> "The best part of beauty is that which no picture can express."
>
> Francis Bacon

There's something more. A disturbing side effect of focusing only on product and looks. Right now, our notions of beauty are shrinking. As the language of beauty is becoming limited, so too is our ability to express it. Even in matters of appearance, a kind of *"one body type suits all"* mindset is setting in. If your basic inherited appearance doesn't fit, forget it.

Would you like to see more diversity in what's considered beautiful? It bothers me to think good people are being made to feel so bad. To me it is a denial of so much that is wonderful in our diversity. Our ancestors, as survivors through tough times, passed on their genetic make-up. Giving us their best, their legacy became our inheritance. That's why I believe hating our height, essential build, or face shape is so destructive. It rejects our physical existence. Our pride in our heritage is being denied.

So, what's to be done about our disappointments over appearance? As an old Yiddish saying puts it, *"If things are not as you wish, wish them as they are."* Simply, it's not what you have that needs changing. Just your way of seeing it.

What we center our attention on we see the most, don't we? Unacceptably big bulges or embarrassing bony bits stand out when we zoom in on them. With a well-worn patter of put downs, we secretly go into our regular rehearsal of guilt and disappointment. If that's true for you, I want to say, *"Snap out of it."* Accept that you deserve some respect. By turning your attention toward living more beautifully you will become freer. Time to reduce the rubbishing and claim beauty back. Time to know *you are okay.*

Deeds for Making a Difference

A bigger picture view of beauty relies on you bringing out your own personal qualities. It's not so much something that happens to you. You must deliberately let your best keep happening.

Think about your view of beauty and what you can do to unveil it. With endless possibilities, beauty is as diverse as all the most promising dreams you can conceive. It presents you with both opportunity and challenge. Through deciding and doing you can make your moments ordinary or extraordinary. The power of choice is yours.

So where to from here? I have chosen five personal aspects: kindness, dreaming, self-acceptance, being loved, and family. Each, is of enormous impact. For this reason, I will explore them further in this book. Some will matter more to you than others. But they represent parts of life that will have an ongoing influence on you.

Consider what you relate to most and choose to do something beautiful with it. Go with your gut feeling and target those areas for particular attention.

1. Kindness

Travel the world, and its relevance is immediate. Kindness is the mark of any civilized society. Through its generosity, much ill will is eliminated and many hardships overcome. Communities of every kind can develop a personable feeling. Be it in the giving or the getting, kindness boosts our sense of belonging.

The same is true in our immediate circle. Kindness builds

> *"Beauty is everywhere a welcome guest."*
>
> Johann Wolfgang von Goethe

togetherness through nurturing and affirming. Whether known or unknown as an internationally recognized figure or simply as a tender mother, we can all influence with kindness.

2. Finding and Following a Dream

So much has been said in the past century about the importance of a dream and for good reason. There's nothing like the consuming passion of inspiration to energize us into action.

Achievers speak of being motivated and how it keeps lifting them above their situation. Living more fulsome lives, they challenge us to find our own yearning to make things happen. Though dreams made real are marvelous, the real magic is in putting in the effort to make them come true. Pursuing something we believe in is actually the dignifying thing. By getting a bigger view of life and what we can do, dreaming makes the sweat of our efforts sweet. In more recent years that seems to be vanishing from our thinking.

Start asking about inspiring *dreams*, and it's likely that most people will only volunteer their *wishes*. Like hoping for a lottery win, they're not so much dreams to reach as fantasies to escape to. Missing the vital work ingredient guarantees missing not only the results but everything satisfying on the way.

Great dreams have importance for their influence. Through finding inspiration in something grand, your efforts become more than worthwhile. If they have something noble to them, they too can translate into greatness. When it does, your passion can become a beautiful cause.

3. Self-accepting

Being comfortable in your own person is the basic foundation for happiness. But many of us keep struggling to accept ourselves as we are. Obviously amplified by the perfect body myth, self-doubts are robbing our lives of precious pleasure. So, the daily bombardment of mixed messages about our self-worth takes conscious effort to overcome.

Finding your feet in this way will always be challenging. But unlocking your abilities demands it. This kind of journeying inwards offers rich social benefits. For instance, knowing you are okay as you are means you can't help but bring ease and poise to your relationships.

4. Being Loved

On the face of it, being loved is the one element we have least control over. But its driving force is so persistent; its power cannot be dismissed.

Being loved as we are is both a comfort and an inspiration, isn't it? Healing a multitude of hurts, it provides a safe haven when we feel low. When pitched, tossed, and buffeted by problems, knowing we are loved gives us solace.

When it's lacking, our joy is dulled and our emotional world adopts a brittle feeling. Life feels grim. Because we thrive on being loved, we become restless in its absence. It is a hunger, I believe, nothing else can nourish.

> *"If you would be loved, love and be lovable."*
> Benjamin Franklin

So, though elusive, this theme is crucial. Whilst working on being loved might seem overly self-focused, it cannot be denied. The challenge is that we must rely on others to give it.

Hoping like crazy that a certain someone will become smitten by our affections is far too difficult to control. Perhaps just as well.

If people don't respond to the best we try giving, then we face that as a valuable truth. It hurts but less than building relationships on false hopes does.

Choosing what to give out, though, is within your power. Happily, some people will appreciate you for it. Whether it reaches a particular person or not, expressing our love is still the best method. Done unselfishly, it's empowering.

This is not to say that your love won't be ignored or even trampled on now and then. Giving yourself genuinely takes courage. If you are in a hostile environment, letting your giving go further afield can sometimes be your best coping strategy.

Turning this need of ours into tender encouragement for others is also a beautiful response. By building appreciation and intimacy, we are creating a sustaining realm: a love that's not just about us but about sheltering each other.

5. Upholding Your Family

Bringing life together more deeply means investing in our relationships. Not living as takers, forever leaning on others for help. But *giving* to make our presence encouraging. Letting our qualities shine through by appreciating the people closest to us is a private work of beauty. Difficult as it is, building a rich reserve of goodwill within our family is a high calling. True, pouring out our finest, year in and out, might show little. Or, it could yield a fabulous harvest.

But this is about purpose, not getting. Making family your first and foremost love can never be successful if it's done for reward. Only belief can drive this kind of investment.

> **"One of the greatest diseases is to be nobody to anybody."**
> Mother Teresa

Being willing to face all of the challenges of family is a sign that we are ready to grow. Facing problems swept out of sight under pressure and distraction requires daring. Committing in the face of open hostility takes perseverance. Not to mention putting up with lousy conditions and being taken for granted.

Yet, despite it all, the paradox of pain, disappointment, and strain is that they are not our ultimate obstacles. With purpose and an abiding commitment to act with beauty, we can face the flak pretty well. Dealing with the dysfunctional and the downright nasty is best done if we can see beyond the moment. To me, surviving all of this in family life is the ultimate apprenticeship for handling the rest of life.

Building family ties triggers a cascade of flow-on effects. Seemingly, small-scale or even invisible, family is about big outcomes. In you, in them, and the people you all become. Upholding your family could even be your biggest contribution yet.

Regardless of how you choose to live, these five facets of life will inevitably have a huge bearing on who you become. They are inescapable. Yet they also offer you the best opportunities to give your efforts lasting influence. Not just as a means of making you feel more fulfilled. But by doing something vital where your practical influence counts.

Discovering Beauty As Is, Where Is

Whatever our priorities, beauty is not about making everything twee, just so, and all *"happily ever after."* Residing in our wishes, thoughts of perfection rarely last long in the real world. They persist only in our imaginings.

> *"The best and most beautiful things in the world cannot be seen, nor touched ... but are felt in the heart."*
> Helen Keller

Magical thinking always expects to find easy ways to clear away our hurts and troubles. But beauty does not do that. Nor does it need a clean canvas. Beauty can grow in the muddle of the moment, to create something lovely with your life. Just as it is.

Even in a mess, true beauty is transforming. With it we can help turn hurt into hope and failure into bright future. It is the vital ingredient that has its roots in the reality of our situation.

Thankfully, wherever you happen to be living, it's abundantly available. Frequently, it's obvious. Or maybe it's hidden beneath a whole lot of ugliness. Either way, it will move you in unexpected ways. So keep opening yourself to its influence.

In the full flavor and appetizing aroma of a lovingly prepared meal, in the lingering affection of a well-planted kiss, or in the soothing calm of a well-tended garden, remember that beauty encircles us in the simplest of things. Each does something words clumsily stumble to say. Bringing quality to our life, such things have the potential to excite us. If we sense them.

Most likely, our obstacle in discovering the beauty around us is indifference. Being overly familiar, we stop noticing. Somehow, things can seem to be better elsewhere. Sometimes they are. More often, we just miss seeing the best we already have.

> *"There is nothing insignificant in the world. It all depends on the point of view."*
>
> Johann Wolfgang Von Goethe

Like relationships, there are bound to be complications. Searching for perfection is a dead end road. Promising everything, it leads away from the satisfaction that only comes from being human: imperfect and uncertain.

Beauty is often portrayed as precise and pure, which automatically counts us out. Given Utopia and ideal worlds are not for this life, we need a kind of beauty which we too can share. With qualities to inspire us, we need it to bring out our best right where we are.

Somewhere close by there's that kind of beauty: the type that can touch you with its magnificence. Making your words turn feeble as you try expressing your feelings.

Giving you a certainty that defies explanation, it's a beauty that nourishes a feeling of belonging.

Merely brushing against this kind of beauty is enough to inspire you. What is so heartwarming is that we find it so close to home. When everything keeps insisting beauty is either out there, by exclusive appointment, or in an economy version available in six easy installments.

Instead, the beauty that surrounds now is both free and freeing. Nourishing and satisfying, there's no more of it in stores than there is anywhere else.

Start actively discovering beauty and you're likely to find it in astonishing places. Letting your heart be touched by the good you detect means that beauty then becomes yours. Take it with you. To share.

Chapter 2

Awareness Reflection Action

"Happiness is a butterfly, which when pursued, is always just beyond your grasp, but which, if you will sit down quietly, may alight upon you."

Nathaniel Hawthorne

Getting a sense of beauty that's bigger than a magazine spread is one thing. How do we *keep* being conscious of a bigger view? To me, it's by recognizing beauty's potential to bring us together, building self-respect, and enlivening life. Fortunately, this comes naturally because something within us reveals it.

Possessing two remarkable powers, you have an unlimited talent for beauty. What are your two talents? I call them *revering* and *kindling*. We use them often. But because we don't notice them, or the power we have to wield them, they are mostly misunderstood.

"Let us not look back in anger, nor forward in fear, but around in awareness."

James Thurber

Knowing your two talents, therefore, unleashes your ability to have a more beautiful life.

Building your awareness and deciding on making the most of your moments are essential steps for putting beauty into action. Reflecting on what matters to you develops your capacity to express it.

Bringing beauty into real life relies on the degree of our self-understanding. Our thinking, not the circumstances, decides the qualities we apply to living. That's why awareness and reflection are central to a beautiful life.

Giving the best we have to share completely relies on our beliefs. How aware are we of our surroundings and ourselves? Do we think well? And how often does beauty feature in our thoughts?

Through awareness, reflection, and action the beauty of your ability becomes obvious. Your particular focus will reveal it in your own unique way.

Revering

So how do we develop our capacity for *revering*? Well, try this as Step 1. To sense more beauty, relax. You might think taking more notice of things would be first priority. But first, I recommend relaxing.

We see, we feel, taste, smell, and hear. Yet, what we are sensing is a kind of simplified replay of what we've known before. The very first time as a child, you nuzzled a rose, inhaling its intense perfume; that first sight you had of birds gliding silently high overhead; or your first experience awakening to golden rays of sunlight streaming through your window: each represent moments of subtle but intense beauty that flooded throughout your curious, young mind.

Then, gradually, in growing up, repeated experiences formed patterns. Instead of wondering at the shimmer of sunlight playing on water, the pattering of rain, or the presence of trees, they barely capture your attention. Having built up a vast bank of sensations, it's easier drawing from your vast memory bank of similar experiences than taking notice afresh.

So if we suddenly see a rainbow we immediately start checking our thought library and *yes, we've seen one before*. Lots in fact. *Yes, okay, there's a rainbow. Hmm, pretty*. We see but only to compare.

By referencing back to previous recordings, we step away from fully living in the moment.

Try this: Start drawing a tree on a piece of paper. Unless you're a bit of an artist, you'll notice your finished product doesn't exactly look like a real tree. Instead, we mostly draw symbols which represent all the trees we've seen before.

Relying on assuming and creating symbols has the benefit of allowing shorthand processing of what we've encountered. But this comes at the expense of enjoying the full-bodied experience. We're here, but we've got other things on our mind.

Even if we're asked to notice more, we tend to keep repeating our patterns of experiencing. Only now, frowning with concentration, we try harder to make our assumptions more accurate. It doesn't work because assuming hinders sensing.

> *"The ultimate value of life depends upon awareness and the power of contemplation rather than upon mere survival."*
>
> Aristotle

That's why I encourage you to relax, assume nothing, and appreciate that this moment really is fresh. Though it may feel completely familiar, the reality is that this very minute is new. Presuming now is just a variation on yesterday is something of an illusion. So be prepared to question the similarities. Right now you are laying down a different layer of your life.

Sensing things afresh is the greatest discovery tour we can take without a ticket. Parking previous knowledge to one side, we can begin reactivating rusty awareness. Sensing details that we haven't noticed for years is bound to be awkward at first, but persist. Try experiencing as much as you can of what's around you, like you did as a kid. Feel the chair you're in, the weight of your arms resting, and the tension in your neck muscles. Try not to talk. Even avoid thinking because it's distracting. Just open yourself to feeling and experiencing this new moment.

Being in the here-and-now like this is the artist's secret and a child's world. Knowing through encountering is the live concert version of life. Raw, moving, and uncut. Next comes a sense of appreciation which I call *revering*. It's akin to becoming aware. But *revering* implies something beautiful in ourselves we express in response.

Getting a hug from someone you've missed for so long, you feel the warmth of skin. Touching their body, you are conscious of the comforting sense of contact. Their arms wrapping around you communicate the length and strength of their emotional embrace. These give clues to the depth of your relationship.

Now imagine that same hug differently. Having just discovered they've been lying to you, all of your sensations are being decoded differently. Instead of joy and satisfaction, your hug feels deeply discomforting and you want it to finish.

That's why translating, in part, relies on what's inside us. *Revering* is the good that we make from our open senses.

> "Without something beautiful to appreciate we cannot live."
> Allan Smith

Potentially appreciating each signal coming in is an *attitude* that delights in beauty. By discerning with admiration, the consciousness of *revering* allows beauty to be seen everywhere. Through it, we are capable of interpreting the unexplainable.

Without this remarkable gift, I believe our identity would be blind to beauty. With it, we can translate the wonder of the intangible and even amplify its magnificence.

Like a muscle, our capacity for *revering* can keep being developed. Just as willingness enlarges it, tuning our experience of people toward appreciation brings out beauty otherwise hidden. Fresh awareness stimulates it.

You could expect *revering* to increase in an atmosphere of pleasure. Yet strangely, difficulty and lack can seemingly offer greater gains. Pain, deprivation, and even suffering can have enhancing effects. Why? Because hardship helps us see more of what matters and the intensifying effect of contrast brings clarity.

Giving yourself moments of quiet helps build your ability. Refocusing your *in-the-moment* awareness provides the groundwork to help you reflect.

Some will appreciate particular activities to boost their *revering*. Others will prefer becoming more aware though life as it is. Believing that new activities can be a good stimulus, I've made a list of a few ways to resensitize you. Otherwise, please yourself by finding ways that suit you…

- Go exploring each week, discovering something different. Perhaps visiting a park, art gallery, wood, or beach. Look especially for natural places.
- Seek out handmade work and look for the beauty of its finish and craftsmanship.
- Visit a place of worship. When you're there, just sit and drink everything in with reverence.
- Listen to your favorite music without doing anything else (Except perhaps dancing!).
- Find a peaceful spot and settle in on your own. No phones, screens, or interrupting sounds. Just observe the stillness and your willingness to stay in the moment.
- Spend time playing with little children, pretending, chasing, and sharing in their fun.
- Get some digging done in the garden, planting and pulling weeds. Feel the sun on your back and respect the work of your hands.
- You can do similar things with embroidery, cycling, jogging, or whatever! Just be sure to tie your focus to the act of doing something physical.
- Spend a few hours listening out for kindness in people's voices. See their expressions, smiles, and gestures. Watch how they show affection. Skip any urge to judge them. Just observe and appreciate.
- Practice savoring beauty as you eat by taking time to revel in the taste of each mouthful you take. See the color and presentation of everything before you. Feel its texture as it reaches your mouth, pretending you've never eaten anything like it. Savor the moment as much as the food itself.

There are umpteen ways of building your *revering* ability. So find something different to do each week without going far or spending too much.

Then, after doing these things, try describing three different features of the beauty you encounter to promote your focus. By doing this, you are building your *revering* skills. The more beauty you recognize, the better you get at engaging with it.

Healthy *revering* of our relationships and surroundings has an uplifting effect. There's reason to find greater respect, and preserve beauty for its own sake. As a cure for boredom, encouraging curiosity, and openness, *revering* has no equal. And it all starts when you relax.

Seeking Beauty Out

Etch this into your memory: the vast part of your beauty rests in your mind. Forget your complexion or your loveliest possessions. Beauty's characteristics are determined by the quality of your awareness. By appreciating more, beauty's influence can fill your thinking. By *revering* you give it wings.

Although it's all around you, beauty needs *you* to liberate its wonder. You are the secret to discovering the beauty around you.

That's why beauty is best experienced firsthand. Experts may draw your attention to something exquisite, helping you appreciate its finer points. But revealing its beauty relies on *your* response. If you perceive nothing then its beauty cannot exist for you. It can only be revealed by the delight of those who know its presence.

This means that it is helpful being with people who value beauty highly. The effect rubs off on us in a positive way. Much as the opposite is also true. Those who dismiss beauty are prone to belittling your appreciation. Trapped in a world of ugliness, they have learned to see beauty as pointless vulnerability. Being hell-bent on surviving, they forget beauty's influence. By shutting down their gift, I believe they are also suppressing themselves.

Getting freed from a hostile mindset requires deliberate steps. First, sheer will, then open suspicion of intentions, ultimately giving way to healthy questioning to break from ugly habits of thinking.

Becoming more in life, I believe, is a natural desire powering our progress toward maturing. However, this common tendency has, to some extent, been hijacked by lifestyles replacing growing with *getting* or *impressing*.

Beauty and personal development are close partners. But it is hard to find them in harmony when life is driven by possessing and domineering. It's as if self-seeking opposes merit.

Of course, beauty remains regardless. But difficulty in *revering* compromises experience, giving rise to wanton destruction, excessive criticism, and hostility.

Caught in this mindset, I can only keep feeling unfulfilled. Hopping from one thing to another to find happiness means it keeps on disappearing from me. Despite all that I have, the fleeting rewards of pleasure seeking are never going to be enough to satisfy.

Rarely knowing beauty in the simplest things would only compel me to look elsewhere. So that by buying, possessing, and consuming I could try finding some contentment. But that's never going to be enough for me. Not only do I want more, I actually need it.

Compare that with moving toward beauty for its own sake. It's a complete shift of emphasis. Wealth, or lack of it, is irrelevant. Status makes no difference either. Being neither bad nor good, they are separate to the deeper theme. How aware are we? Do we reflect on the beauty and ugliness of how we behave? If we do, what action do we take to live deliberately, according to what we hold in high regard?

This is why looking for beauty is both an inward and outward journey. Not so much of getting but becoming. Instead of trying to find it in some obscure and mystical place, though it can be there too of course, I suggest trying closer to home.

Think of your favorite piece of music. How does it go? Imagine it playing in your mind right now. What about your favorite food? What does it taste like? Can you smell its flavor by thinking about what it looks like?

Now take a few moments to picture the place you would love to be at this moment. Putting the book down, close your eyes now, and dream yourself there. Having now done that, briefly give thought to someone you really like. See them in your mind, and ask yourself what it is about them that you admire most.

Somewhere in each experience is something beautiful to explore, isn't there? Distinguishing their beauty, we value them. No matter how humble or even how priceless, it's our perception that makes each important to us. Kept in our memories, your *revering* makes their beauty come to life as often as you choose. Your connection is the lynchpin to its expression. It's a part of your beauty-making ability.

By growing your awareness, you see more and feel deeper. It's like becoming more conscious has a way of changing everything around you. You might be doing the same things, but you bring something different to your encounters. Not least, the capacity to open up to the possibility of beauty so close that it cannot be seen. How wonderful then to discover such a tremendous joy!

Witnessing moments that would otherwise be lost and claiming their delight is like finding hidden treasure. Most often, the things we lose stay lost to us because we no longer bother looking for them. That is why continuing to seek out beauty is *essential*. Finding helps you live beautifully right now.

Perhaps the most personally challenging area of *revering* is appreciating yourself. Take your body image. Excluding miracle makeovers, only a greater sense of awareness is ever going to change things that bother you.

Seeing as it belongs to you, at least take a look over your anatomy. Perhaps it's not the body you'd prefer. Maybe you have uncomfortable feelings about it. But, however you feel, every part is there, real, and part of your own story.

Living in your body, it's easy to take it for granted because much of its cleverness is concealed. Tending to assess ourselves by the exterior, we barely do it justice.

Even if, in the back of your mind, you know your body is immensely complex, you probably pronounce judgment by how it looks.

Unfortunately, looking is a poor tool for discerning the worth of this amazing equipment.

Being independently mobile, your body also comes complete with its own energy processing, sensing, and interpretation systems. It can travel over land, in water, and handles high-speed travel in cars, bikes, and planes. Capable of fully manipulating an extraordinary range of tools, your body also has onboard bio-protection and self-healing functions. To top it off, it's even capable of reproducing.

So far, scientific research has only revealed a fraction of its secrets. But we already know nothing made comes anywhere close for sophistication. The externals barely hint at all of its powers.

That's your body.

Naturally with something built for harsh conditions, we don't even use half of all our features. So, for most of us, using it to the fullest is something of a lost art.

Mothers, for instance, know that during childbirth their bodies possess incredible power. Athletes too have a respect for their body's ability to perform. They, like dancers, actors, and artists, have an affinity for the body's versatility. Respecting its exquisite possibilities for meaning and movement, they get a glimpse of its infinite potential.

Read about some of the latest discoveries on the human body—your body—and be amazed. Yet, although we have such an incredible ability to think and learn, we treat our physical selves with surprising ignorance. No matter how we may appear, we should refuse to accept a peasant mentality about our physical selves. Because it's your home and can do so much, your body deserves utmost respect.

Perhaps our contempt has more to do with our lack of respect for ourselves. Stretch marks, spots, fat, and wrinkles pose an easy target upon which to pin our self-disapproval. Doing the once over, we scan our sags and lay blame on our bulges. Sighing, disappointedly, many of us feel the frustration of being trapped inside anatomy we don't want. But consider this: how much easier is it to accuse lumps and bumps than a lack of appreciation?

When you come to the point of recognizing good in your body

just as it is, you are truly growing in awareness. That same respectful understanding gives you graciousness toward others too.

The greater our perception, the more certain we feel in *revering*. Just as seeking beauty is easier with a mind given to beauty, a beautiful life is the natural expression of a beautiful mind.

Reflecting and Questioning

Whatever our thinking style, beauty is not about making everything *just so*. Nor is living more beautifully a neat skipping trip through wooded dale and hills to "*Happily-ever-after-ville.*" Living a life well lived is too demanding for that. Real world beauty, whether delicate or grand, possesses a quality that's clearly profound.

Living a beautiful life in the here-and-now implies some kind of self-examination. It means giving yourself a regular attitudinal check up. Doing this well sometimes needs help. Like a physician unable to heal herself, we also benefit from the guiding of loyal friends, family, and counselors.

Being prepared to ask the awkward questions about our own behavior has value. Call it mental *housekeeping*. As a preventative, seeing what drives us can also free us from some of the emotional baggage we're carrying. Sometimes, good professional counseling can be worthwhile. Compared to working out our problems by ourselves, a good psychologist can help to fast track our mental spring-cleaning.

Whether we have problems or not, wise listening and advice exposes us to healthy thinking. That in itself is a good way to get a bearing on how we *think* we're doing.

This fits in with a life willing to make new discoveries. Revealing what you're like behind the way you are is just the beginning. Creating fresh approaches to handling old problems in your relationships comes next. It's like tapping into know-how you never knew existed. Both in you, and immediately to hand, the riches of discovery are there for the asking.

That's why I like open questions. They're a sign of maturing. Not like loaded questions intending to manipulate or questions asked with no interest in knowing. But the wondering kind, that allow for new learning.

If you're frequently feeling unhappy, this is a reason to start asking more questions. When you feel chronically tired and wonder why there's no time left for you, dare to ask yourself what it is for. Are there reasons worth believing in? If not, how can you make things change?

I wonder if you feel like this. Has anyone acknowledged the difficulties you have been under? Or has it all been swept away as just part of life?

Waiting for help from others won't do. You need to break free by directing your own journey. Daring to find ways true to you is also about deciding what needs to go. Asking yourself and reflecting on the importance of tasks could help you decide. Getting rid of things that don't deserve your life sacrifice can be more than liberating. This simple act can be an experience in pure release.

Having a young family, we thought we needed two cars. But the payments were increasingly becoming a strain. So asking ourselves whether we could get by with only one car led to us decide we should at least try. Compared to the pressure of repayments, balancing our needs for the next seven years was a happy compromise. But it took willingness in asking, and answering, the question to make it happen.

Now, I know this sounds obvious, but I believe many situations have answers we never discover because we fail to flex our questioning ability.

It's something you need to think through with honest awareness: the repayments that keep you forever owing or the mounting credit debt that's too scary to face. What if we began cutting our coat according to our cloth? How would it feel appreciating more of life by reducing our slavery to stuff?

If the things that bind us are worth less than our being, isn't it time we put life first? Why not find new ways to ease our burdens and live better differently, especially if the things that bind turn out to have dwindling value?

This kind of exploring is about rediscovering your potential amidst all of life's assumptions. Waking up to options gives us newfound freedoms only you can discern.

Question your load. Like a hot air balloonist, ask yourself what deserves releasing to lift you higher. Beliefs that hold you back, perhaps? Or maybe too many commitments are bearing you down? Whatever you do, have, or use, start asking about its purpose and focus on doing what you choose.

By asking, you allow for possibilities you are yet to discover. Plus, questioning gets us thinking more quickly than telling.

Asking lets us liberate our clamped down feelings, giving us permission to feel, think, and see. This liberation is also why wise educators value questions so highly. By asking, we allow for new possibilities. In a sense, we are flexing our awareness. New ideas upon which to reflect facilitate new options upon which to act.

Beyond all the *oughts* and *shoulds*, being conscious encourages possibility. Could beauty have a greater meaning than most people think? And how can anyone live beautifully if the only gauge is a gleaming mirror and some tired clichés? What makes a life beautiful anyway?

Within the questions lies the answer.

Failure Behavior

Discovering your beauty invites you to go past how things look to bring beauty to life. For we all carry small seeds of failure behavior, often without knowing. When they start sprouting, the tangle blocks our best from coming out. So, it also means facing the junk within.

Failure behavior typically shows up in our habits of blame and self-limit (*"What's the point? I'll never be able to do that," "It's not my fault," "Forget it. I'm too fat/thin/tall/short/something..."*).

Where do these failure behaviors come from? In a way, they're a form of self-protection, unbridled. Blocking or deflecting possible rejection, failure behavior aims to ease the pain of feeling inferior.

Becoming a black belt at avoiding criticism, I used to do it a lot.

But, over time, that kind of defensiveness only left me feeling worse. Now I know. Stepping up to the plate and facing my own inadequacies offers more control.

Quitting on ourselves and fearing failure are obvious enough. But fearing success? Getting that way comes because our life paths are scattered with difficulties. Much like burrs and seeds attaching to us, gathering self-doubts and troubles holds us back. Hampering our freethinking, they make feeling defeat seem normal. Like weeds, fear of success keeps choking the good we're growing.

Living with beauty in mind keeps uncovering these weeds. Against our qualities, failure behaviors seem so small-minded that we can begin to see how they are holding us back. Whilst finding failure behavior is an uncomfortable feeling, it's also releasing.

By becoming aware, we can start removing them.

Dislodging failure behaviors brings you more focus and confidence. Granted, it's going to hurt sometimes. But when you're ready to adopt more courageous and freeing ideas, progress is quick.

Personally, uncovering my own weedy ways was definitely unpleasant. Freeing as it is, there is no denying *honesty* is a keen–edged thing. So expect your self-image to receive a few nicks and cuts here and there. But it's worth it. To get rid of the tangle and see yourself for the good you can do is liberating. Awareness opens you to enjoy a richer experience of life and love.

Like plants needing pruning, we need to remove the mess in our crown now and then. Disentangling cynicism and deception from our thinking helps all of us to flourish. Over our lifetime, we bear all kinds of fruit, some sweet and some bitter. So why not choose to produce a harvest of the best we can grow?

Too Big for Our Britches

Building a bigger view of life might risk adopting a cocky attitude but only if we ignore the influence of beauty on ourselves.

Honesty sees the source of our vanity whilst *heart* and *giving* healthily keep turning our attention away from ourselves. No, the cause of arrogance is not influence. It's primitive ego. Out of check, ego assumes command by demand. Either drunk with attention or overcompensating to get it, there is no beauty in selfishness. Easily getting out of hand, self-obsession is just another version of failure behavior.

Remembering that, despite our gifts, there is something very basic about us all is also part of the reality check we need. As wonderful as our talents are and as clever as our biology is, our thinking and actions are bound to ordinary things. Maybe that's just as well. Dictating terms, our bodily needs put balance to our amazing capabilities. No matter who we are, we are each a surprising mix of remarkable and plain. If ever we begin kidding ourselves we should be as slick as the shiny things we buy, we begin to unbalance. In that one simple conceit, relationships and identities get lost and suffering starts.

Pegging back and sharpening our senses helps us understand that our basic self needs to be grounded with calm.

The Healing Power of Calm

We all benefit from calm moments, but ask and most people declare it's impossible to find enough time. Maybe it's a definition thing. If moments of calm require hours of lying back sipping a drink, soft warm breezes, and feeling relaxed, forget it. How often is that going to happen? When we're busy working, ferrying kids, shopping for groceries, preparing meals, keeping house, and chasing our tail, it won't follow. Nor is it practical.

So let's look at things differently. For starters, calm moments don't need to be hours long. Nor do they require the aligning of sun, moon, and stars to get them. Calm can literally be the space between conversations. Considering calm in the frame of micro breaks might seem extreme, but if that's all the time you have right now, use them.

Watching people work, as part of my role in work-based rehabilitation, has been revealing. Despite repeatedly wanting time out, in reality people rarely let themselves take breaks. There's a gaping breach between wanting and doing. Partly, it comes down to priority.

> *"Fear less, hope more, eat less, chew more, whine less, breathe more, talk less, say more, hate less, love more, and all good things will be yours."*
>
> Swedish Proverb

Giving pause between activities, or even simply between thoughts, builds space in a busy day. It might only be a few slow breaths, but it allows you to pace what can sometimes feel like a runaway train.

Choosing to give yourself moments of calm is a small decision that can build a worthwhile habit. Simply wishing for time out when you are busy won't change anything. Instead, focusing on the benefits of calm moments builds our opportunities to catch our breath.

So, now and then, clear your mind of thoughts as well as you can by concentrating on a physical action. If chattering thoughts keep rushing through your awareness, try listening to music, staring into the distance, or something similar. The trick is to find something simple that's easily repeatable.

Gazing off into space for a spell, taking time out for a coffee, closing your eyes, stretching, shrugging shoulders, or rubbing your temples can all offer pocket-sized moments of relief in an otherwise tumultuous day. Though minimal, they might just be enough to humanize an incredibly hectic schedule.

With a bit more time you could consider:

- Leaving your work desk for lunch
- Going to the washroom
- Feeding the birds in the park
- Doing some people watching
- Taking a twenty minute catnap
- Enjoying nature
- Going for a run
- Tuning out at the gym
- Praying
- Having a chat with a friend
- Reading a good joke
- Snuggling up to a cozy fire
- Gazing at fish in an aquarium
- Studying a bird in flight or flitting about from twig to ground
- Consciously slowing down your actions and feeling yourself in the space you are in

Each can provide moments of release where we can step away from vigilance, forget responsibilities, and relax.

Can't do any of these things? Then go walking, preferably briskly if you can. But strolling will do too. Go somewhere you've never been for a change. But just go. I highly recommend walking as a great way to connect with yourself, your surroundings, and your physical self. Just as it builds awareness, so it also promotes a calming influence.

Because time out, for any length, is refreshing, I encourage you to let yourself off the hook more. Consider consciously being unavailable for phone texts and messages now and then as a form of *offline therapy*. Switching off and powering down helps put you into the here-and-now of your body space.

Sometimes you just have to disconnect with others to connect with yourself.

Now you might think being busy is the opposite of finding relaxation and calm. But for some people, engaging in high-energy activity hits their reset button. Then, and only then, are they able to move into a tranquil state. So an intense workout, for instance, can promote a period of quiet afterwards that feels immensely relaxing.

Certain activities, like hobbies for example, keep you busy but can be soothing at the same time. Perhaps enjoying your favorite meal, reading a book, or spending time with little children does it for you. Or maybe gardening, games, crafts, or singing. Whatever it is, just be sure to fully focus on what you're doing. Multi-tasking, by contrast, seems to have a tendency of undoing the benefits.

When life is too crammed with things going on to let us reflect, things come unstuck. Though outwardly exciting and perhaps impressive, a life too busy for thinking can end up feeling deeply deficient. Even the most impressive "*I can do it all*" life feels like a cage if over-scheduled and undermined by a lack of calm.

Tranquility, however brief, has healing properties. You need calm to counter a hectic world. Even if the pressure is mostly in our minds, we still need the restoring power of retreat.

These periods take us to a state where we become more

conscious of beauty. Being overwhelmed by demands and task-based decisions, calm counters, letting beauty make sense.

Moments of silent awareness in particular not only reconnect us, they can be transforming. Released from responsibility, if only for a while, we are free to come up with some of our best realizations.

That's why the silence of lying in bed, getting ready to sleep or fully waken, is so valuable. Moments of twilight and soothing calm aren't just down time. They provide us with potential for a special awareness. Connecting our deep conscious state with our resting mind promotes insight and inspiration.

Giving the quiet whisper of your inner realizations room to be heard needs more though, than time out. For the benefits of calm to be felt, there simply is no substitute for quiet. Despite any feelings of discomfort in the stillness of our own company, our personal sense of peace needs this. Evidence is mounting that too much noise not only increases health problems but can even result in premature death.

Health aside, removing ourselves from the torrent of input lets us rediscover something else important: the ability to feel comfortable being ourselves.

Ideally, places to live and work ought to have restoring areas, somewhere that encourages a reflective spirit. Unfortunately, the vast majority of modern buildings offer little in the way of soothing spaces (unless you call the water cooler calming).

Lacking a sense of calm, homes and offices frequently ignore this core part of being human. So, in the blaring media of TV and the rush of *to dos*, stillness has almost become a foreign concept.

I believe nurturing an atmosphere that recognizes our needs deserves thinking about. Whether in your bedroom, your workspace, or simply in your company, the world needs more peacefulness.

Reducing noise and distractions, we can create opportunities for calm that we can control. In doing so we can encourage reflection, giving everyone the best opportunity to discern the beauty of the moment.

This is what I call *kindling*.

Kindling

This gift is blissfully easy to grasp. Just as your appreciation interprets beauty, *kindling* makes it. *Kindling* is your ability to create beauty with action.

> *"To live is the rarest thing in the world. Most people exist, that is all."*
>
> Oscar Wilde

Remarkably, the wonderful power we have for *kindling* beauty into existence is often ignored. But think of it. Right now, by your own choosing, you can personally bring beauty into this world. You don't need more money, better looks, or more anything. Just being who you are is enough.

Most of us think of beauty as something outside of us. Buying it, admiring it, and treasuring it, sure enough. But *creating it*? Don't you have to be artistic for that?

Whether you think you would be good at it or not, I expect you are doing it already. Just that you haven't been thinking about it this way. Considering everything you are doing, the scope for expressing beauty in your tasks is vast.

There is no realm where it cannot go. No person who has ever lived who did not need it. Despite having beauty to give as we choose, we are scarcely aware of it. What's more, this incredible gift is unique to each of us. Nobody else has your version to express. No one.

Choosing to act out of kindness for no other reason than itself. Caring with compassion for someone sick or frail. Tidying, and putting things away because you care. Getting things done because you believe in the benefits they bring. Such actions are not so unusual in ordinary experience. By *kindling*, however, we turn each small thing into something significant.

A teacher I once met gives up her yearly vacation time to serve as a Good Samaritan in Cambodia. Giving her time and money, she does it as an expression of her faith. Taking it upon herself, she contacts locals to find where she can be of most help. Not only does she love doing it, but it's immensely fulfilling.

That's a big thing for one person, isn't it? But there are so many scales of *kindling* we each can choose the best scale to fit.

When a family falling on hard times discovers a secret delivery of groceries at their door, somebody *kindled* that moment into existence.

Or, wearied by a hard day working, someone makes beauty happen by surrendering their bus seat to another tired soul.

Whether we do something or nothing, every action is a statement to each other and ourselves. In a hard-edged world where it's easy to shut down our feelings, this gift is potent.

Being unaware of this bigger view of beauty would mean missing the focus it brings to what we do. But being sensitized to it, we can discover our influence. *Kindling* puts fulfillment into relationship.

In beauty we have somewhere to shelter. Riding out our storms of frustration, anger, and disappointment, we have a reason to be calm.

Instead of inferior feelings, we can also claim our personal strengths. Making our life count, wherever and whatever, is precisely what you were born to do.

Though we may not have met, I do know something about you. I know you have what it takes to bring warmth and encouragement into the lives of others. With abilities that haven't been fully explored, you have a whole lot of living to discover.

Sure there have been things in your life holding you back. But you can't keep waiting for things to be right. Now is the time to bring out your best with boldness.

Kindling beauty needs no timetable. Only a definite desire smoldering within you that wants more in life.

Maybe things haven't been as good as they could be for you. Maybe you have good reason to feel disappointed. Being drawn to beauty, perhaps your inner self is making an important connection. Beauty, by its nature, increases our awareness of kindness and encouragement. Hungering for them also has a way of feeding our desire to give them.

When you are tuned to see goodness, all that is beautiful in you seeks expression. But it's true we are a mix of many things, both wonderful and dismaying. You and I are full of contradictions. Being ambitious for more, we hold both noble and selfish hopes. But I believe this restless wanting emerges because deep down we know we are capable of more. We feel the pull of possibility, tugging at all our limitations.

Channeling that changeable urge into *kindling* acts is the way we open our life to the possibility of deep satisfaction. *Kindling* nurtures the contentment we need for happiness.

Striving solely for ever more power and possessions pours people's attentions into a hoarding mentality. Distracted by the process, much of their creative ability for beauty gets lost.

Instead, deciding to express your beauty rewards you with something more. Knowing you have the power of beautiful influence, you ask yourself where the best places for investing yourself are. Doing things that matter gives you reasons to live more beautifully. In the process, you end up connecting more closely with others, the moment, and yourself.

Being so familiar with the plainness of our ways, I believe we tend to discount ourselves. Even writing ourselves off. Heedless, we are mostly blind to our incredible influence for good. Which is why grasping the wealth of your talents is so exciting. Like discovering you're the heir to a great inheritance.

I want this to sink through every pore: you *deserve* to express all that's good in you. Others need you to. By daring to make something beautiful through your actions, everyone benefits. Like the butterfly effect, small acts of *kindling* have unforeseen, rippling effects.

Creating what you value is nourishing for your self-respect. Being gracious builds your dignity. So sharing whatever you can be proud of energizes you.

Consider what you are already doing. Remember when you were especially gracious to someone recently? What happened? How did you feel?

Like *revering*, this sublime strength of yours is one your greatest assets. Yet, putting beauty foremost is perhaps only a slight adjustment. You are simply doing more of the good you have always done.

> *"I know who I am and who I may be, if I choose."*
>
> Miguel de Cervantes Saavedra

Magnifying your intentions with focus makes *kindling* a natural priority.

Even when ugliness is hurled our way, we have the power to release what we choose. We can repay, measure for measure, through the unthinking ways of ugliness. Or, we can dictate our responses with beautiful purpose.

Deliberately expressing beauty prevents life from being mediocre. No matter how plain and unremarkable we may consider ourselves to be, this small choice carries an ounce of greatness into every situation. Why? Because of the difference in the way we do things.

Notice how we all keep looking to see what others are up to? Then, by comparing, we measure ourselves. Our social checking behavior is so sensitive and ingrained; we cannot help seeing what everyone is doing.

That's what drives our influence. In a way, *kindling* ups the ante.

Seeing expressions of genuine kindness in our community influences everyone's thinking. Coupled with encouragement or courage, even the most minor events can become powerfully, even strangely, moving. So much so that coming across a couple of courteous drivers, a kind storekeeper, and a forgiving friend can trigger an overwhelming feeling of wellbeing.

Though we are naturally attuned to spot trouble, our capacity to appreciate tranquility is remarkably intricate. Even if it mostly lies dormant, we can awaken this gift. Through *kindling* we can achieve results as far-reaching as they are heartfelt.

Fortunately, it's easy to start with what we already do, particularly with the little things.

Creating Simple Beauty

Doing small things in a great way is within everyone's reach. Instead of setting the bar so high that you put off doing anything at all, consider what you normally do. Creating good is doable when we keep it simple.

Forget about waiting for the right moment and ideal conditions. Keep turning your beautiful thoughts into action where you are, with what you have. Break through wishful thinking and accomplish more with your present realities.

Simplicity seems too hard to accept for some. Feeling as if more is better, they complicate and over-elaborate life to death. But I believe in finding your simplest expressions of beauty. Practicing them often will give you the confidence and satisfaction to do more. Deliberately cultivating habits of appreciating and creating beauty will create their own priority.

Whilst expressing quality is enriching, merely waiting for good things to happen in life ignores our talents. By creating beauty right now, you are making life work. Your relationships, environment, and manner all await your transforming touch. Thinking differently automatically gives life a fresh significance. Ordinary moments can now present themselves as opportunities to appreciate and generate something beautifully worthwhile that you and others can enjoy.

I know some people will think, *"Who cares about all that? I couldn't care less so long as I get what I want."* But what do we want? The answer has layers. Wanting more things, power, and pleasures, we also want to be loved, appreciated and do something important. Deciding what will give us ultimate fulfillment is a function of growing. Some, preferring not to amount to much, of course, never do.

Nothing, I believe, plumbs the rock-steady depths of fulfillment like beauty. It doesn't matter where you are or what is lacking. You can bring beauty into existence in the bleakest of places. Daring to choose kind words, sharing effort, and expressing courage makes this beauty real. Giving without strings and allowing others to be themselves breathes fresh air in the stuffiest of surroundings.

How many times have you been left feeling unheard, uncared for, and taken for granted? In each of those moments, it was beauty that was missing.

We are shortchanging ourselves if we believe life is all in the long-anticipated big events. Life is in every minute. Recognizing it and creating quality in the small moments is the secret. Even when understated, beauty is an irresistible force. It has drawing power.

> *"As you see yourself, I once saw myself. As you see me now, you will be seen."*
> Mexican Proverb

Wherever you are, actively searching out beauty and offering kindness are both purposeful and healing. Rather than shabby thinking, we can enjoy ideas that are rejuvenating. Not by trying to be nice, impressing, or gaining approval, but genuinely being aware and desiring to see beauty in your normal experience. It builds you, polishing you in the process, so your qualities can reflect in the lives of people you know.

Instead of becoming a clone of someone else, this is about being the real self you respect. Your calling card expresses what you are learning to love about yourself. So make your mark by sharing beauty in your own unique way.

You can expect that some will keep being unimpressed. But beauty is not about pleasing everyone. Beauty is a case of tuning in and conveying to build your own self-respect.

Sense beauty in the biggest and smallest of things. Choose simple ways to bring beauty where it's lacking. Dignify your life with it and listen deeply, concentrating on both the spoken and the unsaid. Insist on respecting others for their qualities, not their trappings. Be warm, putting people at ease with acceptance.

Keep building better work habits, expressing leadership and reliability. Keep thinking about what you can do beautifully in the here and now. Give it full expression. Whether in work, or doing all the other things you do, appreciate beauty, and let it be your mark.

Chapter 3

Revealing The Seven Strengths

"Be as you wish to seem."
Socrates

Redefining Ancient Knowledge

Throughout time, certain qualities have been inspiring to people, communities, and nations alike. They have been the bond uniting families, building belonging, and keeping nations stable and prosperous. We keep forgetting that, despite all the confusion and turmoil, we all share a commonality: our humanity. Despite the vast variety of customs, beliefs, and technologies around the world, our basic needs remain the same.

Worldwide, the major religions keep drawing followers to their unique beliefs, symbols, and practices. Some of us like to lump them all together, thinking they say more or less the same thing. But given the distinctions in their core spiritual beliefs, that can't be true. Lumping all faiths together would also be deeply affronting to many followers. Quite literally, it would be against their religion.

Yet, despite all their many differences, they *do* share some things in common. Together, they all uphold a number of powerful virtues.

Great societies continue honoring these qualities too. By valuing them as signs of civilization and noble success, each culture pays tribute in their own way.

Threading through our interaction, these truths of influence wend their way through everyone's life. Regardless of customs, beliefs, and technologies, these attributes still keep determining our caliber.

Consider the surprising similarities between these virtues:

Christian Virtues	Hindu Virtues
Respecting all people	Respecting
Being honest	Being honest
Having compassion	Showing compassion
Having self-control	Possessing self-control
Exercising servanthood to others	Giving hospitality
Being humble	Demonstrating self-discipline
Forgiving	Being tolerant
Acting with wisdom	Having wisdom
Being generous-spirited	Supporting non-violence

Islamic Virtues	Buddhist Virtues
Being truthful	Gaining awareness
Showing compassion	Showing kindness
Showing self-control	Showing self-mastery
Showing respect	Developing servanthood to others
Being patient	Developing a peaceful mind
Forgiving	Forgiveness
Being humble	Expressing humility
Expressing selflessness	Being selfless
Gaining knowledge	Seeing through appearances

Judaic Virtues	Confucian Virtues
Being honest	Being honest & trustworthy
Having compassion	Being humane to others
Having self-control	Applying dedication & persistence
Respecting dignity of all people	Earning respectability
Remaining patient	Patience
Expressing forgiveness	Loyalty and forgiveness
Being humble	Modesty
Acting with wisdom	Showing wisdom
Gaining knowledge	Being benevolent

Sikh Virtues	Modern Humanism
Recognizing the equality of all	Expressing kindness
Sharing and servanthood	Learning through education
Showing compassion	Upholding peace
Upholding peace through non-violence	Respecting the rights of all people
Being honest	Caring selflessly
Supporting freedom	Cooperating
Developing wisdom	Promoting freedom
Working hard	

Valuing Truthfulness

Now, of course, there are more virtues and more worldviews to be followed, but you can see these beliefs share surprisingly similar themes. Mind you, just because they are central doesn't mean all followers live them out. Whenever they ignore them, clashes, disharmony, and much tragedy occur.

Whether we have a faith or not, putting the power of these potent elements into our lives is transformational. That's why I encourage you to apply them for yourself.

Crossing all boundaries of culture and religion, these recurring truths are an enduring legacy of wise knowledge and experience.

Bringing them together into seven key words, I call them The *Seven Strengths:*

> 1. Giving
> 2. Fortitude
> 3. Honesty
> 4. Heart
> 5. Releasing
> 6. Visioning
> 7. Wisdom

Their power belongs to all of us, no matter what our spiritual or cultural heritage. Combined, they give us the opportunity not just to live well but to live beautifully.

Beauty in Action

Doubtless, some people will mistake these as merely sentimental ideas. But, in practice, each is powerfully life affirming no matter what the circumstance. Each strength has endured throughout the ages, helping humanity cope with the ugliness of strife and natural struggle. As mere words in a list, their influence is easily dismissed. But as truths to life, their expression represents some of the most powerful concepts any of us will ever learn. Denied their influence, our relationships would wither, and our society would simply stop functioning.

> *"We shall never know all the good that a simple smile can do."*
> Mother Teresa

So commit these strengths to memory using whatever way works best for you. Picturing something that reminds you of each truth can help. Particularly if you try making it funny, scary, or even a little bit silly. Remember them because relationship beauty depends on their meaning.

Think about them in your own life. How much of an impact

have they been having on the way you've been treated? And, how comfortable are you in applying them?

The substance of the Strengths might seem overdone to some. But think through what matters most to you. Cast your mind back to those times in your life when you experienced strong feelings of gratitude for a kindness given. Or when, despite the cost, you stood up for what you believed. Maybe you have had a personal battle forgiving someone close. Or perhaps reflect on how *The Seven Strengths* are weaving through your life right now. Expressing them not only offers direction; it gives you beautiful influence upon the world.

With infinite options for expressing this, you and I can bring beauty to life any way we choose. But if you're not sure how, here is a little list of 101 ideas to get you thinking. Pick any that suit, remembering to exercise your good judgment to avoid misunderstandings. Most importantly, enjoy being yourself and expressing your best:

1. Work well in your job because you are making a statement about yourself.
2. Say thank you to people at every opportunity and mean it.
3. Let someone off the hook.
4. Give someone a shoulder or foot massage.
5. Run a bath to pamper someone you love.
6. Find something you like about someone you work with and casually mention it in conversation
7. Give somebody a smile with genuine warmth.
8. Accept the imperfect.
9. Leave something for the future: kindness, heritage, heirlooms, and wisdom.
10. Practice keeping calm until you feel more in control of everyday life
11. Forget your self-focus sometimes and completely direct your awareness to whomever you are with.
12. Leave personal attacks out of anything written. Write like your emotions could get into the wrong hands and be misinterpreted.

13. Remember beneath the harshness of a quarrelsome person, they really want to feel respected and valued.
14. If you don't like the social rules, consider changing them
15. Drop gossip that is unkind, nasty, or undermining. It's a dead end that keeps us down.
16. Get to know people you already know, only better, by assuming you know nothing about them.
17. Live now. By all means, plan for the future, but make today matter.
18. Change what you can that really bothers you and release the rest.
19. Now and then, try switching off every communication device in your home so you can switch off too.
20. Concentrate on feeling aware whenever there is an in-between moment. Sense your breathing. Touch surfaces with your hands, and feel the air on your skin. Give your senses maximum power. Then reflect on the experience.
21. Buy or find flowers for enjoying and sharing.
22. Develop the art of actively listening. Concentrating for a whole minute, give your complete attention. Then work up from there as you are able.
23. Tell a friend or family member how much they mean to you, without seeking a response.
24. Post a card or letter to someone telling them how much you appreciate them.
25. Send a newsy letter to someone you haven't spoken to in ages and tell them you've been thinking of them.
26. Have a helping mindset.
27. Practice giving praise to people, based on what you like about their personality, without embarrassing them (e.g. *"You are so conscientious, Robin. Who taught you to be such a hard worker? Was it your parents?"*).
28. Be genuine so that your actions mirror your true beliefs.
29. Take a walk every day to connect you to where you live, and help you think.
30. Contemplate nature. Become aware of life around you such as it

is, developing respect and understanding.
31. Find a place where nature surrounds you, where the sounds you hear are all natural.
32. Whenever you say something bad about somebody, counter it with five compliments.
33. Better still, if you feel inclined to severely criticize a person, stop. Then, if you can, immediately switch gears by doing something really physical for half an hour. Consider what's beneath your criticism and what you really want to achieve.
34. Dare to speak kindly but honestly with someone close about something that's been getting between you.
35. Pick up someone else's rubbish without complaining and compliment yourself for it.
36. Mow a neighbor's lawn.
37. Tuck a few coins into places where school aged children enjoy playing.
38. Send a few photos to a friend or relative to share good times.
39. Give blood at a blood bank.
40. Be wise in your handling of decisions affecting your family at the moment. Make wisdom a priority in your daily decision-making.
41. Give away clothes or other things you no longer use to somebody who could.
42. Respect the dreams and hopes of others, even if you can't relate to them personally.
43. Next time a salesperson tries to sell you something you don't want, let them know you aren't interested, but find a reason to praise them personally (e.g. *"But I do appreciate the way you approached me. Thank you, and all the best with your next customer"*).
44. Treat people coming to your door promoting their religion with respect. Be firm, but treat them with dignity.
45. Pat your children often. For many, though not all kids, a kind touch is shorthand for *"I think you're great."*

46. If someone has a good phone manner tell them. Most often, they will be surprised by your praise.
47. Encourage kids a lot. But always tie it to things they know are true (e.g. *"Well done, Dennis. I knew you'd be quick, because you're such a fast runner"*).
48. Spend a few minutes going through your old photos, and send whatever you can part with to the people in the photos.
49. Send an email of support to an organization you believe in. Try doing it once a week to a list of groups.
50. Whenever you call someone you know, begin by asking if you've rung at a good time. Anyone busy will appreciate your thoughtfulness.
51. Develop a thicker skin. Many an argument starts from misunderstandings. So preventing a few fights could make life a lot more pleasant.
52. Go out of your way to talk about people's good points to others. It's great gossip and it often comes back to people as a wonderful form of encouragement.
53. Give room for people to express their feelings, whether they do or they don't.
54. Many people are shy about their appearance and find real compliments hard to handle. So tell people what you like about their looks in a way that makes it easy for them to respond (e.g. *"Your hair is looking lovely. What do you use to make it so shiny?"*).
55. Raise money for charity.
56. Drop some money into an envelope and anonymously deliver it to someone in need.
57. Donate time and effort or money to a cause that you hold dear.
58. Stop everything and play with your kids.
59. Keep some change handy for people who might come to your door looking for a charitable donation.
60. If you ever get service, don't just tip well. Tell them why you appreciate their efforts.

61. Visit someone lonely and maybe take them for a walk and a talk to bring them encouragement.
62. Volunteer an hour or a day for a worthy cause.
63. Sit down and eat together at the table, without TV, cell phones, or any other media.
64. Wave at little kids and smile.
65. Buy some groceries and have them delivered to someone who really needs them.
66. Hug people in your family and say thanks for being my sister, brother, etc.
67. Remember that heated arguments don't have winners. They have combatants. So let people be wrong now and then.
68. Acknowledge people in your presence rather than ignoring them.
69. Be willing to model *heart* and *wisdom* by saying sorry first.
70. Be as good as your word to let people know what kind of person you are.
71. Offer a seat to someone when commuting to remind yourself what kind of person you are.
72. Bring a host's children a small treat as a way of recognizing them.
73. Help people nearest you whenever you can.
74. Be determined about the things you believe in and show courage.
75. When someone wants to talk with you personally, prevent disruptions. Just focus on them. If you are really busy, tell them you are. Tell them how many minutes you can give them, and if they're okay with that, stick to your time limit.
76. Use your imagination to make things better for someone you care about.
77. Become aware of your inner critical voice and start challenging it.
78. Be loyal to people you have known for a long time.
79. Develop a vision for your future. Make sure it not only inspires you but its fulfillment will lift others as well.
80. Be respectful to all people, no matter how lowly or lofty.
81. Be the first to introduce yourself by name. Include other people's

name in conversation to show recognition.
82. Visit people who are hospitalized to give them care and encouragement when they may be feeling anxious or lonely.
83. Meet your neighbors and get to know them by name.
84. Whenever a past wrong comes to mind, remember the past no longer exists. Let yourself vent your feelings if you need to but in a safe way. Then remind yourself you have the power to forgive others and yourself, so recommit to *releasing*.
85. Do something funny for somebody you know will appreciate it.
86. Be the gatekeeper of your mind. Use *wisdom* in discerning what is worth seeing, listening to, and talking about. Let what you do build you.
87. Where you can, make the most of your moments. Make a chore an act of love, and remember it is important simply because you are.
88. If it fits and you believe it wise, give people what they want.
89. When driving your car, be conscious of people. We may only see their cars, but focusing on other drivers as people naturally puts us into a more respectful frame.
90. Let someone go ahead of you in a queue now and then. They may not appreciate it, but you are making a statement to yourself.
91. Help out a neighbor with something homemade. Or perhaps offer to give them a hand.
92. Demonstrate *honesty* in your work and personal life as a mark of self-dignity.
93. Realize we are all a work in progress and release judgmental thinking before it reaches your lips.
94. Deliberately look for the good around you. Get into the habit of finding something to like in all the people you meet in your day. Even those who annoy the pants off you!
95. Take what you do seriously, not yourself.
96. Turn down your blame gauge and concentrate on making good things happen by your own hands.
97. Give your sense of humor a thorough work out daily. Refuse to

be too serious too often.
98. You already know lots. So now it's time to find out more. Be willing to learn new things and ask questions.
99. Don't trust your ego. Instead, be willing to look a fool now and then for the sake of being more *heart*-filled and *giving*.
100. When others aren't doing what you want them to do, do it yourself and feel good about making things better.
101. Much of what we want to tell others to do is best caught not taught. That's why living out your beliefs says it best.

Signaling

It seems that for the most part, we implicitly feel action defines us. Creating effort from intention, we express ideas. Engaging in activity, we tell the world we're here.

Bringing *The Seven Strengths* to life can sometimes be unintentional. But living a life of beauty generally shows that your deliberate involvement matters. With intention, life naturally has more purpose. This in turn keeps feeding back, creating opportunities for deeper satisfaction. Through *Giving*, for example, you end up affirming yourself.

Whether we apply these qualities or not, as far as the world is concerned we are known by what we do. Our actions define us. People will therefore judge us accordingly.

The outward image that we construct is constantly sending out signals. Through daily interaction, we keep proclaiming what kind of person we are. Just as everyone else does around us. Surrounded by a vast variety of social signals, we are continually immersed in meaning and sub-meanings.

Putting them into words, plans, and activities is our open response. Then there are the many layers of meaning below this. Like the *"come hither"* signal of body language and tone, we express our intentions in intentional, yet mysteriously coded, ways. Like a lingering look or by revealing an inner wrist whilst gently stroking your hair, our bodies are always communicating.

Many, however, go deeper still. Where the signals sent stay below the radar of the sender's awareness.

What makes these layers of communication important is that we constantly rely on them. Making decisions, developing relationships, and finding our way through life goes better when we are more aware. If we're not, then we better be with someone who can do the tuning in for us.

Not only does a greater understanding of each other enrich life, it reduces the risk of sending out mixed messages. Choosing deeds of beauty upfront, for instance, whilst resenting people a few layers down tends to sabotage everything.

What we are sending then needs to make complete sense. That's why being aware of signaling can be such a strong relationship builder.

To me, there seem to be two reasons for poor signaling. One is a difficulty in reading the signs. When we don't get what's being transmitted, we rely on assuming our way through (How many times have you become frustrated by someone misreading your signals?).

Aside from confusion, the effect of feeling misunderstood can quickly become exasperating. Occasionally, it plunges us headlong into resentment.

The second source of signaling difficulties, I believe, is poor self-awareness. Not knowing what we're actually telling people, can severely undercut our intentions. The person peddling religion at the door, for example, may not realize their message conflicts with their pushy approach.

Just like cheesy chat up lines put us off, unless everything fits it fails.

More subtly, people can send out mixed signals like:
- *You couldn't possibly understand.*
- *I don't feel good about myself.*
- *I'm trying to fit in.*
- *Please keep away from me. I'm feeling hurt.*
- *This situation is beneath me.*

...when they're trying to sound upbeat or convince you of something.

Whether loud and clear or silent and secretive, all messages work best when they are tied with words and deeds that match. Being an experienced communicator yourself, you generally believe the unspoken cues. People's physical reactions, you've learned throughout your life, provide the clues to revealing the unvarnished truth.

When it all fits, we can believe what someone is saying. But believing is still a long way from *trusting*.

Trusting goes further, doesn't it? When everything somebody does over time matches up, only then does trust become a real possibility.

So every gesture, word, sound, and position has a subtext. There is always something more in a pause, or a mutter than what face value offers.

Because we are naturally emotional beings, I believe everything we communicate is underpinned by an emotional basis. Meaning, even the most matter-of-fact comments have layers that signal feeling.

By answering questions with a stern voice, my emotional subtext might display a want to sound important. I might be trying to impress you (or even myself). Though a strange thought, all of our day's communication can be plotted with emotional purpose. Meaning, if we ignore people's emotional expression, we completely miss the essence of everything we think we understand.

> "The art of being wise is the art of knowing what to overlook."
>
> William James

Naturally, if people key into our emotional purposes and seem to approve, we tend to like them. If I feel helpless, my signaling will reveal it, a bit like bait. Some will be repelled by the signal without even putting words to their intuition. Others will be drawn to come closer because their signaling matches. Maybe they might feel at home with a kindred soul. They may have a need to rescue, and my looking lost triggers their emotional purpose.

Not that we are necessarily aware of this layer of messaging. I don't believe we mean to be signaling as much as we do. Ultimately, it's impossible not to say something through our body language, tone, eyes, and ideas. From drama teaching I learned that, even when we are staying totally still, we keep on communicating.

That's why it's wise to be deliberate in your actions and let them do the talking. Bring *The Seven Strengths* to life in your own wonderful way, paying particular attention to *honesty* so what you intend to share through your signals will be loud and clear.

Otherwise, we leave our expression open to misinterpretation and misunderstanding. This is only part of the difficulties we share in communicating. We also have the potential to harm for harm's sake.

The Self-harm in Harming Others

Whenever we move away from true beauty, hurt begins taking a lead role. Though a natural part of life, the pain from causing harm is a byproduct of failure behavior. When somebody is caught up in a life of ugliness, maltreating others can even feel good. Yet inflicting harm on someone else has a contaminating spread. What we give out infects us too.

> *"Good can imagine Evil but Evil cannot imagine Good."*
> W. H. Auden

Deeds, both noble and cruel, reflect our lives and shape our identity in the eyes of others and ourselves. By repeatedly causing harm to others, people reinforce a powerful statement about themselves. Not only do they imprint their self-knowledge with action, but others confirm their character.

Whatever we say becomes our defining speech. Known by our deeds and the words of our mouth, we carve our own reputation. What others recognize, we confirm. This can be wonderful or disastrous. Getting a reputation doesn't take long, which is why harming others coerces us into a corner. Causing trouble risks earning a label others, let alone we ourselves, cannot easily forget.

Nor can we avoid labels by being unknown. Knowing our own actions and the character of our deeds is an unavoidable part of awareness. Conscience can gnaw at us. It can destroy our self-image as a kind of built-in payback for causing harm, reminding us continually how bad we are for the damage we've done.

It follows that those with a shriveled conscience seem to create the most havoc. Managing to get attention and even admiration, they look like they can *"get away with it."* But do they really?

Having little regard for others, they seem to suffer few direct ill effects being cruel. Yet nor do they know satisfaction in fulfilling relationships. Their price is not guilt but a greater personal failure. By repeatedly harming others they keep themselves locked in a pathetic identity.

> **"Science is organized knowledge. Wisdom is organized life."**
>
> Immanuel Kant

Completely incapable of relating well, they lack the ability to live an enriching life. Instead, gathering the trappings of influence, they rely entirely on show. In extreme cases, their cold-hearted ugliness becomes their badge. Being both dangerous and pitiful, they live in what I call a permanent pattern of failure.

Gratifying their ugliness, sadistic people with brutal tendencies exploit others for pleasure. As their primary goal is to dispense misery, trying to broker beautiful outcomes is unlikely to work. To combat this influence, we need to precisely define what's wrong. Recognizing the results of their behavior is a crucial step in defusing their power.

Perhaps you work with someone who gets off on being cruel. Or maybe you have borne the brunt of a family member's abuse. How do you handle them?

Clearly seeing the situation for what it is gives you the power to make better judgments. By working out what's happening, we can profile behavior and communicate it to others. With the strength of numbers, callous individuals start losing clout.

We can also refuse to *own* their actions. Knowing they have a harming problem, they alone are responsible for their intentions and their conduct. It's not easy going, but I believe this is a vital step.

Whatever the circumstance, vetting our intentions through *The Seven Strengths* can also reduce our own tendency to harm. Testing the fabric of our intentions through their qualities sure beats surrendering to emotional whims.

Years ago, Ruth and I had our consultancy repeatedly robbed. A gang casing the area broke in three times in as many weeks. Making a terrible mess, they repeatedly stole vital equipment that we had to keep replacing. Feeling violated and frustrated, it was easy to adopt a victim mindset. Yet, having an important job to do, we all persisted regardless.

In this case, *fortitude* helped keep us true to our role. Working with people with high needs meant handling the impact of damage and theft had to take second place.

But it's totally different when it's personal, isn't it?

Ron, a work associate, had been secretly and systematically abusing his wife Jenny throughout their marriage. Through physical and psychological torture, Ron had turned Jenny's once beautiful life into a nightmarish world of fear.

Tormented by a childhood marked by hidden abuse, Ron's pain kept rippling out. Only now, he was secretly doing the torturing.

When Ron finally cleared out for another woman, Jenny needed the strength of others to bolster her *fortitude* and guide her through. Drawing on their *wisdom*, Jenny got the help she needed to face the ugliness of Ron's abuse. For Jenny to make a new life and finally be free, she required unfaltering support.

We all have situations where things are difficult, don't we? Sometimes our problems are so bad we fear that voicing them will make things even worse. But whatever we go through, we should at least know that support is always a viable option. There *are* people out there who care. People with kindness and understanding to help. Providing we let them.

The way I see it, we need to refuse to let the ugly actions of others define us. Clinging instead to the guidance within *The Seven Strengths* lets our best come to light. We all need *wisdom*, whether our own or given. So we should keep seeking it out. Having courage, and applying our own *fortitude* to cope, even when it means just hanging in there, is character in action. Living with *honesty* is unashamedly daring. Whilst, being true to ourselves and refusing to be part of someone else's lies is living life with strength. When we are ready to build new beauty and find new freedom, *Releasing* ultimately makes sense despite the hurt. So keep this thought close: the pain of your past has no rightful claim to your future.

Shockingly Ugly

You and I know *The Seven Strengths* don't magically make the entire world a bright, happy place. Trauma will remain an ongoing part of life for many of us. Knowing beauty doesn't dismiss ugliness. Sometimes it just makes it obvious.

Being conscious of The Seven Strengths will give you a flinching sensitivity to just how ugly humanity can be. Cruelty and destructiveness are clear enough. But high handedness masquerading as superiority is also revealed as abuse and inadequacy.

> *"Avarice hoards itself poor. Charity gives itself rich."*
>
> German Proverb

Greed and callous disregard start looking tragic against the light of *giving* and *heart*. Flaunting proud vanity looks weak against *honesty's* strength. All that's meant to impress and oppress is plain to see.

Those hell-bent on power will keep tearing strips off others. Vengeful backbiting, rumor spreading, and humiliation will continue, often unopposed. People will endure it, stomaching it all as if they are powerless in the face of it.

But living as we believe gives us a reason to live well. As people with a common bond, we know our actions count. Releasing the past, we can give something of beauty to the people of the future. If we choose, we can even dedicate something precious for people to appreciate a hundred years from now. Or we can simply live right now with all the courage of our convictions to resist such ugliness.

Like most societies, I suspect we often like to think of ours as civilized and clever. But the fact that we dedicate so little of our efforts to realizing our beauty is telling. Being too busy doing, it's hard for people to see that unless they choose to live with beautiful strengths they fall victim to everything else.

A supportive and encouraging community does not start with our leaders, media, or experts. It begins with you and me. Then our friends, family, people we know, and beyond. Like a jigsaw piece, we belong. Being part of the whole picture, your part is integral. We are, each of us, original but similar. Without you, the jigsaw that is your community can never quite be complete.

Our Self

I suppose that's why switching our identity to fit an image is such an odd concept. It comes, I believe, from a misunderstanding of self that leaves us feeling uncomfortable about being real. Switching personality staves off having to deal with ourselves.

> *"Wisdom is the supreme part of happiness."*
> Sophocles

If we had a stronger notion of the importance of self, things would be different. By seeing ourselves as beings of dignity, originality, and capability, we could be more conscious of our influence than our image. Understanding the way we act, speak, and engage is central to a beautiful life. Not concealing our weaknesses but building our character just as we are.

Then, instead of the rise and fall of selfishness, we could all see how puny and unsatisfying thoughtless grasping is. Like the little boy seeing the emperor without his clothes, all would be revealed. Even the hidden jealousy of tut-tutting the self-seeking of others would be made plain.

We would see egotistical behavior as weakness rather than flamboyance. Money, celebrity, and the length of our title would no longer be a permit for posturing. Displays of vanity and conceit would be embarrassing admissions.

Celebrating the exclusivity of self-centeredness would be laughable. The message that it's somehow good to be a bighead wouldn't wash. We'd simply see it plainly for what it is and start looking elsewhere for inspiration.

How different life could be. Self-obsessed individuals, filling screens with their imagined greatness, would actually have to do something useful. Criminals would stop getting interviews and publishing rights. There would be a shift away from fame at any price back to respect for achievement. Not status but performance.

For lack of any other way, we look to the law to contain viciousness and cruelty. Rules also increasingly appear to be enforcing socially acceptable behavior too. They seek to maintain so-called political correctness. It might sound good in principle, but I have my doubts. Enforcing dignity by regulations doesn't work very well. Resentments remain, only deeper and more disguised. Hiding anger in obstructive resistance has even become a badge of honor for some. Their silent aggression as ugly as everything they oppose.

> *"Those who are free of resentful thoughts surely find peace."*
>
> Buddha

Good laws and standards are vital in helping us combat some of the outcomes of social ugliness. But legislating or imposing character will never work. Like a contagion, disharmony takes over people's thoughts, goading them to find other ways to cause hurt and harm.

That's why there will always be ugliness. What we need are ways to deal with it. Manifesting *The Seven Strengths* is, I believe, the most powerful, life-affirming response we can make. By applying them to our own situation we are making a statement about what we will stand for and what we won't.

Thanks to our signaling behaviors, we are making a host of social statements. About what we like, where we fit, and what we believe. Like a billboard, you and I are on display. We all are. Only most of us don't quite know what we are conveying.

A Shared Journey of Dreams

Despite all our differences, our passions and longed-for dreams reflect our culture. So it's no surprise that even our goals have a lot in common with at least some people.

If you hold a dream close to your heart, don't be surprised if someone else shares it too. It seems to me that though you are a one-off, your ambitions are evolving from what we share. That's a good

> *"Let us endeavor so to live that when we come to die even the undertaker will be sorry."*
>
> Mark Twain

thing. Even if people around you are less than supportive, somewhere, someone understands and believes in what you want to do.

Find them if you can. Or simply get busy bringing your purposes to life, and the word will get out.

Noble goals need expressing, and who better than you to live them into action? Like fruit that only flourishes in season, your dreams have their timing too.

Letting them germinate and grow is the first step. Then start working to tend them, putting in the effort to stop them shriveling on the branch.

Of course, goals that satisfy only ourselves are ultimately self-limiting. But truly beautiful dreams produce satisfying fruit everyone can share. They become something more because sharing multiplies their satisfaction. For lasting inspiration, I believe, dreams must bring beauty to others. Which explains why dreaming of becoming a multimillionaire is okay if it benefits others too. But if that desire is tied to selfishness, it can lock us into selfish patterns, forever preventing fulfillment.

Take a look around a typical bookstore and you'll find dozens of *"How to Be Rich," "How to Slim,"* and *"How to Be Better than Everyone Else"* books. They make an impressive wish list. But if that's all we ever aspire to, then we are missing greater adventures. Doing something worthwhile that stirs and uplifts others is to truly dream big.

Putting *The Seven Strengths* into action with the passion of your ambitions is totally different. Magnified many times over in the lives of others, these dreams make an outstanding contribution.

Throughout history, I believe these motivations have made a lasting impact. As a byproduct, they have turned ordinary people into extraordinary leaders, influencing the thinking of generations. Turning common attitudes towards higher hopes, they embodied many if not all of *The Seven Strengths*. Happily, their legacy is still with us today.

During the 1800s, the western world underwent dramatic upheaval. In the face of terrible distress and enforced cruelty, a new compassion and inspiration also started surfacing. Completely unknown people began paving the way, helping ordinary folk find kinder, more humane ways of living.

One such person was Clara Barton. Born in Massachusetts in 1821, Clara became a humble schoolteacher at the tender age of 15.

When the US Civil War began she was deeply affected by the slaughter of battle. Being compassionate and intelligent, she felt distress for the many soldiers terribly wounded in battle.

So, tirelessly, this otherwise ordinary woman took it upon herself to do something. She began raising people's awareness by marshaling support to comfort injured troops.

Later, Clara went on, bringing help to wounded further afield in European conflicts.

Eventually, on returning home, she set up the American Red Cross, establishing its headquarters near the White House in Washington, D.C.

A keen supporter of women's voting rights, Clara's dedication to service in difficult circumstances earned her the title *"Angel of the Battlefield."* One newspaper summed up the sentiments of the time by going as far as saying Clara Burton was *"...perhaps the most perfect incarnation of mercy the modern world has known."*

At a time when women were considered little more than chattels, another unlikely visionary was changing the course of history at the other side of the world.

Remarkable for her *fortitude, heart*, and *visioning*, Jane Franklin made the perilous sea voyage from London to Van Diemen's Land (now known as Tasmania) in 1819. Having encouraged her husband to become governor, it was Jane's own support and initiative that began transforming the colony. Championing the underdog, she was soon despised by the landed gentry of this southernmost outpost. Her ideas were so modern they were considered outrageous. Yet despite their suppression, Jane persevered.

Becoming the most travelled woman of her era, she worked

> "Let yourself be silently drawn by the stronger pull of that which you really love."
>
> Rumi

tirelessly to give ordinary people greater opportunities. Improving conditions for maltreated convicts, Aborigines, and destitute mothers in this far-flung colony, Jane paved the way for a brighter future.

Helping rename the colony *"Tasmania,"* Jane Franklin single-handedly opened up new land for farming and created much-needed jobs. Combining her passion for exploration with her *heart* for people in need, she used her position to bring hope and inspiration to a remote outpost of the British Empire.

Later, when her husband John Franklin disappeared seeking the Canadian North West Passage, she organized and led the rescue attempts. Her bravery, character, and capability were so remarkable one British scholar was led to write, *"Lady Franklin was a woman of idealism and great mental activity...determined to assist in the creation of an infant nation."*

What made Clara Burton and Jane Franklin so remarkable was not their looks, prestige, or luck but their decisions. By applying their visionary *fortitude*, they made things happen.

Paving the way with these strengths, we rest on the achievements of great people everywhere. Some like Eleanor Roosevelt, Helen Keller, and Mother Teresa, for instance, are widely known. But there are so many others who, by turning their everyday lives to noble cause, have become inspiring heroes.

If you haven't already, I encourage you to find some heroes in your life. You and I need them. They may be great people of history or simply great people on your street. Discover them for yourself and find the truths that have made their lives great. Letting their influence spur you on, keep doing those things that make you proud.

Borrowing their passion and extraordinary vision, you can dare to make your life count for more. Not that you need to be a hero. But I believe you do want to live a great life.

Real living isn't like the movies, is it? It's not a one shot, give it all you've got, reach for fulfillment. Instead, it's much more down to earth.

Getting up in the morning, frizzy haired and vague, we're still deciding how we will be today. Moment by moment, we keep deciding. Reacting to what's happening, we can go any way. But if we have a noble passion to express, each moment has direction.

Giving in to an existence of passive pessimism, I believe, is just what Benjamin Franklin was talking about when he said, *"Some people die at 25 and aren't buried until 75."* During those times when you stop hoping, you feel like you're amounting to nothing special. That's when we need our heroes. By sharing the greatness of their dreams, we can continue our own journey.

> **"Do your little bit of good where you are. It's those little bits of good put together that overwhelm the world."**
>
> Bishop Desmond Tutu

Persevering with goals is the thing that gets us across the line. Too many people wistfully quit by focusing on their failures and blotting out their experience. But what they miss seeing is that their previous attempts have just been warm ups for greater and grander things.

Sharing the beauty you create can be the simple product of impulse: no more difficult than a kiss or a smile. But deliberately steering your life with beauty beckons you toward a richness of possibilities. Revealing *The Seven Strengths* risks a chain reaction. Following in the footsteps of heroes before us, we have the right to inspire and live a life worth living.

Chapter 4

Beautiful Meaning

"Ever more people today have the means to live, but no meaning to live for."

Viktor Frankl

Ever since I was five, I can remember wanting to make people feel happy. Helping people laugh or smile made me feel good too.

Knowing what drives you is a liberating thing. Being mindful of what makes you tick lets you feel comfortable in your skin. But how do you do that?

I've had various times in my life where I wanted to run away from myself. I even tried. But there's no use being anyone else. Aside from being a poor fit, it never feels right.

Having thought about this over the years, I believe what you really need in life is to *know*. Not so much the meaning of life but the meaning of *you*. What is it that you can do with yourself that really matters?

That's why this chapter is about getting to grips with your values and discovering who you are beneath all those layers of being mature and adult. It may or may not be obvious, but it's worth thinking about. Working this through is important.

After all, finding out who you are meant to be is central to living a beautiful life. Discovering it transforms a chore-filled life into a life of experience. Life rich with meaning puts everything in place. Even our yearning for happiness.

Happiness...Now!

Surf the Internet and you'll see it everywhere. One of the great motivators in life is the pursuit of happiness. Whether seeking pleasure or deep contentment, we want life to *bring it on*.

So, what makes us happy?

> *"What everyone wants from life is continuous and genuine happiness."*
> Baruch Spinoza

Not good fortune alone, it seems. Even winning the lottery won't make us more satisfied in the long run. Prizewinners, it turns out, adapt quickly. Like the first flush of joy from your last pay raise, the pleasure begins evaporating the moment the rest of life sets in.

Some researchers believe we even have a happiness set point, a level where our general spirits keep returning despite all the highs and lows of life. So over time, they say, no matter how appealing fortune and fame can be, our happiness stays the same.

But there's more to being happy than fun, isn't there? From personal experience, you already know it comes in two forms:

1. The type you get with the pleasure of buying something new.
2. The satisfying kind that comes from feeling deeply contented. It's the kind of happiness that only expressing your best or engaging deeply can give.

Perhaps you could say the first is about getting, whilst the second is about *giving* (You can see where this is going, can't you?).

Happiness in thrill form has a way of fading faster than we'd like it to, doesn't it? Compared to the gladness of deep satisfaction, it doesn't go the distance. To be sustaining, happiness needs purpose. Add a dash of self-reliance, and happiness even becomes a statement of character.

Expressing love and thankfulness in your relationships gives you a warming feeling, doesn't it? You could spend the same amount of effort just having a good time on your own. But the thrills won't last or be anywhere near as nourishing unless they're shared. Pouring your energy into something or someone you believe in and feel connected to wins hands down. Why? Because a good relationship intensifies pleasure and offers the potential for greater fulfillment.

People keep searching for pleasure wherever and whenever they can find it. Even if short bursts are a second-rate swap to the lasting joy of abiding contentment, they'll take it. Yet at the same time, everyone keeps longing for deeper fulfillment. That tells us something.

Restlessness might be a flaw, but it's also a clue. Our yearning suggests we're made for more than what we can find in shopping bags or queuing for feel-good experiences.

Though settling for much less too often, we hunger for satisfaction. Why? Because our need for meaning is deep. It draws us just as the intimate connection of beautiful relationships fascinates us. It's enough to keep us turning the pages of a romantic novel or gazing glassy-eyed at the cat and mouse games of lovers played out on the big screen.

That doesn't mean our whole life's fulfillment is hiding in the impulse of romance. All long-term relationships matter. Being with people we care about is what we seek. Through them we get a sense of place, anchoring the meanings we make with belonging.

That's why I believe we're better off ditching the takeout mentality and working on making our relationships last.

As ever, quick fix thinking is pushing us to look for contentment under the wrong rocks. Easy answers with immediate appeal deserve to be questioned. After all, instant gratification is an easy sell. Getting top billing, it earns huge profits, which is why whole industries keep offering us every short-term thrill imaginable. Wanting, we are not content to wait. We want it all *now*!

But constantly feeding our impulses is training whole generations to endlessly hunt for happiness. When fast fun runs out and the parties end, what's next?

Escaping emotional pressure with runaway pleasure-seeking can,

> *"Joy can be real only if people look upon their life as a service, and have a definite object in life outside themselves and their personal happiness."*
>
> Leo Tolstoy

of course, be a wonderful stress release. I do it too, now and then. But because I have a life rich in purpose, running away all the time would be undermining.

When life lacks meaning to hold onto, letting go isn't hard. Lack of purpose is the reason, I believe, people keep falling into patterns of disengagement. Missing personal meaning fans the flames of drug and alcohol addictions with a vengeance.

Falling into habits, it's easy to tune out, to depend on getting a buzz with the pop of a pill or the swig of a drink. Pleasurable diversions seem to help us cope, giving us vital time out. But the more we rely on pressing the escape button, the more life loses worth.

Increasingly, needing to give daily life the slip just to feel fine is a sign life isn't going well. Disconnecting becomes both a symptom and a cause. Evidence our life needs reshaping.

First, to find any lasting contentment, you need to focus on meaning that matters to you. The deeper the better.

For instance, in each of our family bonds and friendships, whole realms of riches are waiting to be discovered. Even if family breakdowns are blocking the way, there is purpose to be had in these relationships. Finding answers and alternatives, though, could call for creativity.

Connecting with people we know, and building new bridges is a good place to start. Oh, and I highly recommend spending time with older people and children. Who better to see us for who we are?

Finding people who love you is one thing. Learning to better love those you've long known is another. Yet these relationships, in particular, have the defining strength to lift us to better things. Why is this? I believe it has something to do with connecting with things that are more durable than how we feel. Facing the familiar with good grace is a grounding experience where we need to handle the awkward realities of relationship. But doing so gives beauty an even more profound touch. Willingness to look directly at what we would rather run away from lets us dare to believe in ourselves.

Today, with little guiding purpose in a daily sense and options galore, people get lost. Insecurity, apathy, and self-doubt are crippling our ability. Yet, the qualities of beauty are right here. With them you can work things out no matter what your situation. Reassuring in their timeless good sense, they put it all into perspective.

Despite having every form of entertainment and distraction at our disposal, we want more. Satisfaction beyond pleasures cannot be denied.

Thanks to our brain chemistry, the hunger for pleasure will always deliver a bumpy ride of ups and downs. At their most extreme, our happiest hormones will keep surrendering their supreme highs to gravel-biting lows. Just as night follows light, it's both predictable and a poor way of living well.

Considering there are times when grief and sadness actually make more sense, there's good reason to experience your emotional range. Forget the calls to be *happy, happy, happy*, 24/7. Being alive is far more intricate and involving than hyped up happiness allows.

Though funerals are typically somber situations, my father's triggered a gamut of emotions. On one day mourning gave way to hilarity, switched back to heavy-heartedness, then finally left us set upon bittersweet reflection. We each did our share of grieving in calm, anger, tears, and tenderness.

Letting our true feelings come out, I somehow felt glad because happiness is infinitely more than merriment.

Lasting happiness depends on the meanings we make and how they affect our real world decisions. Outlooks, whether high or low, are peppered with lingering emotions. Like your very first kiss, your last day at school, or the moment you began falling in love, each emotion is tied to moments of meaning.

Gathering our own vast collection of memories, we sort them out. Ones to keep and ones to bury. Plus all the memories we forget we had until something happens and back they come.

This sorting is determined by how we think now. For instance, low self-image willingly pulls out the worst moments, justifying who we are. Memories of achievements are quietly suppressed.

Like feeling time capsules, choosing to remember what we will releases those emotions again. What we choose to recapture most speaks about our state of mind? Contentment at a day-to-day level finds its denial or release through *purpose*. That's why consciously choosing meaning is so vital to your happiness.

Being Yourself for Good Reason

Be yourself. How many times do we keep saying it, get told it, and try being it? But what is *being yourself?* What is so special about it? And why do we need reminding to be ourselves?

Funnily enough, we probably know more about the Sun's properties than we do about being ourselves. Gathering data, we can measure and describe its mass, energy, and movement with great accuracy. But you? You are a lot more difficult to describe.

Forming their own opinions, people closest to us believe they know. We probably do too, at least sometimes. But though comparing everyone's views would build a good profile, it's naturally going to be fuzzy. Changing to accommodate different people, we bring out different features. You are a different person to a child than to a parent or partner. But it all kind of fits doesn't it?

When we say, *"be yourself"* what we really mean is be your *comfortable* self. The person we know that we like and love with the qualities we recognize and appreciate. That's what I believe being you is about; perhaps unpredictable at times and hard to define. But the essential you is who we want to be with and enjoy.

So what makes being you so important? Think about your last job interview or meeting and you instantly know. Having the presence that comes from feeling comfortable in your own skin conveys confidence. Your thinking is clearer, and you can listen more carefully.

Being yourself can be an awareness boosting state. Relaxing, it's easier to direct your attention outwards. Instead of worrying about your breath, tight pants, or whether you're coming over right, you can concentrate.

Being yourself is being you at your best even without doing much of anything. You simply inhabit a zone where you feel right being who you are. Connecting with yourself like this lets you handle your surroundings with confidence.

How confusing, then, that we keep losing it. Remember the last time you told someone you care for to just be themselves? What was happening? Most likely, they were worrying about some important event. Perhaps they were trying too hard not to show how unraveled they were.

Times like those we all do well being reminded.

Reminding someone you believe in them and they need to be true to themselves can have a reset effect. That is, of course, if they're listening. Chances are, if they're too uptight, snapping back to feeling calm and collected is too difficult.

We need time to pause and think through what's happening. Getting the better of our feelings might mean talking things through or going for a walk. Dealing with our physical response is the thing. Whether by distracting, calming, or processing, coming back to ourselves puts us at ease.

Finding that sense of balance you get by being yourself is worth thinking about as your day unfolds. Getting a firm sense of what it feels like is helpful. Becoming more sensitized to when you start leaving your zone is powerful.

Exploring what being yourself means specifically for you is useful too. People, chronically hurting, sometimes inhabit a damaged sense of self. Being themselves might require stimulants or sedatives to bring them there. In those situations, being yourself can actually reduce opportunities for feeling at ease.

This highlights the importance of maintaining *honesty* in our relationships. By gently supporting and guiding, we can be each other's barometer.

That's why, when it comes to simply being ourselves, it might not

> *"Those who wish to sing always find a song."*
>
> Swedish Proverb

be so much a case of forgetting but more a sense of not knowing how to be in the first place. Just saying *"be yourself"* and things will be right may not be enough. If we exist in a realm of second-guessing and self-doubt, the way to feeling safe in yourself gets blocked.

I have met so many people burdened by self-anxiety and a gnawing self-disgust. They are suffering this distress because they don't know how to be themselves. Having no poised calm or self-assurance to retreat to, they are in torment, trying to escape from themselves.

Perhaps it's a paradox, but striving to live a beautiful life is not going to bring you this peace. That's because beauty is not about forcibly striving. True, creating beauty is about doing. But it comes best when your spirit is at rest with itself. Doing your utmost to make others feel good whilst living your own life in turmoil and misery is not beautiful. It's a tragedy.

Being yourself lets the meanings you make flow richly through everything you do. Without the conflict of warring with yourself, the beauty you know becomes the beauty you can share.

Being yourself allows the meanings you make to be founded on a calm peace. You can build your life on that, knowing the best you do is fulfilling. Having the courage to be yourself then, gives you the ability to make beauty happen.

Knowing Your Values from Your Overlays

Therefore, do whatever fulfills you most. Unusual or common. Supported or challenged. It will never be a waste of time. At the end of your life, which will be better? A life involved in fulfilling activity, or one compromised by all the *"shoulds"* and *"oughts?"*

Growing up, we gather a lifetime supply of obligations, guilt, and emotional bruises. Taking them into our adulthood, they mostly lie hidden beneath all the trappings of outward maturity. But for many of us, it only takes the simplest comment from your mother to bring them out (*"You live like this all the time then?" "We never brought you up like this," "You never did... listen/tidy up/try hard enough/ etc."*).

Triggering a chain of reaction, it can be surprising to see how much raw emotion appears from nowhere.

Known or not, our personal truths are potent. If they cannot consciously influence our actions, they sneak through disguised. Such is the power of our self-beliefs. Doing whatever it takes, we seek to accommodate for them, even at the expense of *honesty*.

Conforming to parental rules, childhood understandings, community, and the media, our certainties are a jumble. Commonly carrying a whole collection of conflicting beliefs, we barely notice the clash. Mishmashed together, they are the basis of our outlook. Defining our view on how and where we fit.

Discerning your personal truths from this patchwork can be confusing. So it's no wonder we sometimes layer our beliefs to suit the situation. There's the *better* do beliefs near the surface, helping us fit in, like exhibiting *proper* church beliefs or assuming the model citizen role. Holding up the values of the workplace might be part of our cover, even though we may have mixed feelings beneath.

So what happens if we dare to go deeper?

Firstly, if you want to start looking afresh at your life you have to do things differently, don't you? If you are prepared to explore your assumptions, I recommend dusting off what I call your *malarkey meter*. Being brutally honest with yourself means not settling for any deception or wishful thinking of any kind.

A good way to begin this exercise is to begin considering the degree to which different things matter in your life.

Using pen and paper, roughly draw a range of concentric circles like you might see on a target and big enough to write inside.

Next, begin listing some of the things that matter to you. Things like beliefs and priorities. Perhaps you'll need to think about them for a while. But as your list expands, try mapping out your beliefs within the circles. Whatever you put in the inner circle represents your core beliefs. Middle circles let you place beliefs that are important to you but not vital. Whilst everything in the outer circle represents what you generally accept but don't particularly believe in.

Compare your views about your family with your public views. What about your thinking on things like politics, nature, and life? What about your work? And where do see the rest of your relationships?

Given all of your beliefs, start looking for any contradictions. You could even draw another circle set and put the same things in it. Only this time, they could be placed by the priority you give them, not how important you believe they are.

When you do this simple exercise, you can see what matters in relationship with everything else. You may want to ask: what needs changing to be true to your sincere beliefs?

Going deeper, perhaps you have beliefs and priorities that, if you were honest, you secretly live out but don't want to admit. Maybe their existence is flying in the face of what you often stand up for. Perhaps you keep them private, believing others would feel hurt.

Confronting as these clashes are, they aren't totally haphazard. They suit us to some degree. Why? Because everything motivating us to act gives us some kind of payback. So if belonging is an important value to us, then choosing to conceal our antisocial behaviors seems the easiest way through. Better off hiding than hurting.

Now I know this might be challenging or just plain hard to figure, but looking at these differences is important if you want a greater understanding of the whys that drive your life. Comparing your real life actions versus what you feel you *ought* to believe can be an eye opener. The reason? Most of us selectively do what suits.

So I want to challenge you with a question. If you hold some guiding viewpoints that you don't want to admit, *why* are they meeting with disapproval?

Somewhere in your real life values is the truth. What you *really* think. Finding them just means untangling them from all of your dutiful *shoulds*.

Which is easier said, isn't it? Bewilderingly disguised as beliefs, we all have plenty of obligations. Along with tons of hoped for wishes and fantasies. But I believe only our truths are wholehearted. Like gravity exerting an attracting force, all your certainties, both secret and open, have a gravitational pull. If your job, for instance, aligns with those definite beliefs, then working feels completely worthwhile. Every day.

How you felt about everything that happened this past week reflects this. From what went on at work to that particular conversation that's been playing on your mind, our core beliefs have a way of coming out and driving our life.

Knowing how your opinions and actions are *meant* to appear to your social circle is a valuable exercise in awareness. By comparing the things you do for appearances against your real ideas you can see the compromises you are making to appease. Giving the deep beliefs you keep permission for expression comes at a price. Meaning demands honesty. But it also lets you enjoy the benefits of living in agreement with yourself.

I believe a beautiful life is consciously true to the beliefs you own. Through awareness and reflecting, even the ordinary feels more fulfilling.

Swap Mumbo Jumbo for Purpose

Being of Christian faith (handy, given my name), I believe there's more to reality than what we can see. But whilst many keep looking for miracles in the weird, I see the wonderful in what we take for granted. Having been made important, the powers we possess are miraculous in themselves. Yet, being too familiar, we ignore them.

Assuming the role of spectators, we look for marvels, and signs of the supernatural. But to my mind, the momentous is already here. It can be found in the gifts of our abilities. Together we can often produce the very answers we've been praying for.

I believe the power for making beauty happen rests in the *purpose* behind our decision-making. We don't need to invoke the forces of the Universe. Our circumstances can benefit marvelously by our

> *"A wise man makes his own decisions, an ignorant man follows public opinion."*
>
> Chinese Proverb

attitude and focus because purpose is a remarkable force in itself.

Proclaiming that wishes will magically manifest thanks to mystic movements or incantations is unfortunate if not plain misleading.

Thinking the magic is in the hat rather than the magician makes us wishful spectators. But you and I are the ones with the magic to make things happen.

Focus is good, but so is firm decision and determined effort. Putting them together is the real secret to making good things appear.

Have you ever wondered why some things we do are so hard? Health and skill aside, it's usually because we don't have a strong enough reason to do them. Take the power of purpose out, and effort becomes half-hearted and full of blame for circumstances.

When a mother yells at her teenage son to clean his room, it's an even bet he'll turn the music up, pretending he didn't hear. A tidy bedroom fulfills her purposes but not his. But when he wants to impress his new girlfriend, suddenly he finds a reason to conquer the mess.

With the power of purpose you can make all sorts of tasks worthwhile and satisfying. You can even influence others.

A positive expectancy of people's ability, for instance, comes through in the degree of respect we give them.

As belief steers our actions it also creates a standard. Rising to it, we encourage others to rise with us. That means it's not skill but the quality of our motivations that decides the caliber of our behavior.

In turn, inspiration gets its strength from the sense it makes. The more meaning behind our motives, the more effort we commit. Which is common sense, right? Then how come so many people hate their jobs and think their life is awful?

People go to work they hate, doing the bare minimum for money. For some, their address is just a spot to sleep and a place for storing, not living in. Spending time with people they don't much like, they keep thinking about moving. Somewhere where the grass is greener.

For too many of us, Life is either a merry-go-round of wearisome obligations or unrelieved monotony.

Why? Simply because many of us don't know what we want. Caught in a whirlpool of conflicting demands and desires, it's natural to become fed up, frustrated and detached. Without enough meaning, people quite sensibly ask, *"What's the point?"*

When times get tough, meaning pulls us through. It's not luck but our beliefs that hold us together to give us the will to carry on. Whether we have a personal faith or philosophy, we depend on that meaning to make sense of life, which is why a life full of purpose is essential to finding beauty in the confusion.

Your Meaning Matters

Let me ask you: How many times have you settled for someone else's purposes and put your own aside? How did you feel compromising your own views? Whilst it's good to be flexible, somehow, we have to keep true to our own meanings.

Not only do you deserve to form your own opinions, having them is vital. With so much flung at us today we need to keep our own head. To rise above it, our greatest power lies in our *choosing*.

> *"Sweet talk doesn't make you warm but sweet meaning does."*
>
> Yiddish Proverb

Consider the media as an example. Taking advertised promises with a grain of salt is a given, isn't it? We know if advertising was about telling the truth many ads would turn into farcical comedy. Despite that, there's a part of us that *wants* to believe. Perhaps it's because their promises appeal to our hopes. Wishing for more we are forever vulnerable to latching onto falsehoods. Tempting potentials hook us, and once caught they reel us in. Over and over. Even when we know it's happening, if the bait is tasty enough we hang on.

Harmless or harmful, the process uses us, doesn't it? Knowing this is happening and talking it up is an important step towards being more mindful. We don't need to be deeply cynical or resentful to question. We just need to know we are being sold and give room for doubt.

As it is, going with the slipstream of convenience is leaving us open to being used and abused by predatory tricks. That's why consciously deciding what matters most makes a big difference. Reflecting on the worthiness of things, consider what you *lose* when you *gain*. To me, that is an essential part of being aware in this *must have* world.

Finding satisfaction according to your highest values gives you courage to choose wisely. It also helps protect you from deceptiveness. The more balanced your sense of purpose, the easier appeals to greed, selfishness, and vanity brush off.

Our vulnerability is highest when we need the approval of others and the promises things offer to feel alright. Yet true beauty reminds us that being all right always rests in our own hands. How we think and act is the real thing. You and I have everything right now to be authentic. We can bring quality to our thoughts and beauty to our conversations. Our limits are not in the disappointing state of our wardrobe or home furnishings; we set them in our attitude.

Choosing to live with purpose connects our days with a grand sense of reason, eliminating so much rubbish. To seek out your own special way of contributing rids life of its shut down numbness. By discovering the beauty you bring, you find the secret of where your happiness lies.

Decisions, Decisions

Real decision-making gets things happening. But what are the features of a real decision? Don't we all make decisions moment by moment? Even when we're feeling undecided, aren't we deciding that we don't know? Similarly, isn't the act of doing nothing a type of choice too?

Years ago I found myself debating this with Roger, an old friend I had grown up with. He felt the idea of choosing to do things in life rather than taking everything as it comes was pointless. I tried explaining to Roger that we can live more richly if we live life on purpose. But he was certain it was better just to let things happen.

Choosing, he said, was far too controlling.

Roger's view was that letting everything unfold by itself makes a better life. To this day, I haven't seen anything in his life to prove it. Barely scraping by, Roger seems increasingly diminished by his situation. Whether he knows it or not, I believe avoiding decision-making is crippling Roger's abilities.

Choices are like switches. Without them, we lose control.

No wonder dangerous cults and abusive partners restrict decisions. Completely denying someone's power of choice is the ultimate form of domination.

Of course, there's the flipside, isn't there? Not only do many of us have freedom of choice, but we sometimes feel we have too much of it.

Building a house, for example, requires thousands of decisions. From determining the depth of a countertop to selecting the height of every handle, the process is crammed with decisions to be made.

When you are weary at the end of a busy day, even the little decisions of grocery shopping can feel too much. Not to mention selecting from the myriad of modern options you have for insurances, phones, computer systems, cars, utilities, etc.

Choosing is a demanding task, taking awareness, thought, and focus.

So perhaps we can be thankful when some things are out of our hands. Frustrating as rules and regulations can be at times, we benefit from the certainties they give. Every day, you comply with rules determining such things as:

- Where and how you can drive
- How you may dress in public
- What you can say

Whether we think about it or not, life in the twenty-first century is highly regulated. In part, that's what you pay your taxes for.

But there is an enormous portion of being an adult that's really up to you, isn't there? You make decisions at all sorts of levels. There are countless little decisions that you make on the fly (*When should*

I come home? What will I wear tomorrow?). Then you have longer-term choices like choosing where to live and work. Between it all you also have the potential to make big life choices. They don't rely on what's going on in your life so much as your own certainty.

Being inspired by meaning, you may decide to dedicate yourself to a cause or take a leadership role for something else that's important to you. No matter what happens along the way, meaningfully deciding keeps you following through. Whatever your circumstances, choosing has the muscle to make it happen.

Now I know we are all busy creating our own circumstances to some degree. Thanks to our willingness and what we focus on, good things *can* come our way. But I believe it's unfortunate when people waste their abilities, preferring to sit, waiting, and wishing for good luck to rescue them.

> **"We can't be at one and the same time half-sure and whole-hearted."**
>
> Gordon W. Allport

Claiming that whatever we focus on will magically make our wishes come true is not wholly true. Yes, focus is good. But so is making considered decisions to get things moving. Combining them with that other wonder ingredient called elbow grease works wonders. Putting them together is the way everything great gets done. When it comes to achieving beautiful results, leaving out decision and effort just doesn't come close.

Removing true decision from our effort guarantees half-hearted results. Incidentally, you can always spot indecision this way. When it's tough going, weak decision leads to excuses and plenty of blaming. When it comes to the big things, determined choice makers keep on carrying on in spite of everything.

The Wright brothers couldn't have developed powered flight without it. Merely being excited about the idea of flying machines would have led to nothing. They had to go and make it happen. Combining their skills in bicycle making, Wilbur and Orville turned their vision into action. Borrowing the ideas of Australian kite designer John Hargreaves, they embarked on countless trials. Through years of careful observation, planning, and action, the Wright brothers eventually developed the world's first steerable aircraft.

Having the privilege of life, we can make it more beautiful with *choice*. But decision minus action is an unfinished formula. Waiting for the Universe to make my dreams come true because I *will* it so is likely to leave me bitter and bent. But the moment motivation falls in love with action, potential can start shaping reality.

Somebody wanting to be a famous singer is excited by their vision. But unless they choose to endure the endless practicing, promoting, and rejections, their focus will fail. Beautiful dreams, minus the character and sweat to create them, will remain in the imaginary realm. The missing magic to decision is *effort*. When it comes to turning inspiration into reality the irresistible power is active decision.

Searching for Self

Some people spend lots of time and expense navel-gazing to find their inner being. But I believe there's a better way.

Seeing your identity is a bit like trying to see yourself blinking. Sure you notice and see it in others. But seeing your own? Despite peering intently at yourself in the mirror, those tricky blinks remain invisible. Recognizing your own identity is equally hard to detect. Perhaps because you're too close to it to fully grasp it.

Finding ourselves, I believe, is best done by examining your actions and the purposes behind them. That's because doing animates your character. Comparing your feelings about the various things you do can at least gives you a good impression. Your elusive self becomes visible through your handprint on life. So obviously, The way you handle tasks, relate, and get motivated is highly revealing.

Knowing what drives you can take time. But by unraveling the meaning behind your actions, you can uncover your best intentions. Not those of your parents, partner, or club. But yours. Untying the strings of obligation lets you peel off the rest. Like removing a mask. Finding your own meaning, honestly and with integrity, requires lots of healthy questioning.

See it best as a work in progress. A journey of becoming more of your true self. Finding your personal purpose is really about *doing you* well. Being truly authentic in your work, home life, and wider relationships.

So discover your beat and dance to it. If you haven't already, start:

1. Taking stock of what you have done so far in all parts of your life (include everything, both memorable and forgettable).
2. Believing that, at the very least, you have potential to do better.
3. Taking your instincts seriously when you need to weigh things up. Even if they are out of step with others, factor them in.
4. Daring to adjust your daily life to fit your inner knowledge.

Now is the time to start doing more of what you believe in and being less tied to what is expected.

Accept personal struggles as part of a normal life and realize they will make you question everything. When they do, look closely at your relationships and what you are doing. In hardship there is a winnowing, so harness it. Decide what truly reflects how you see life. The more definite you are, the more resilient you will become.

Difficulties do more than toughen us. They can give us clarity, even if it's to be more certain we don't have all the answers.

Knowing ourselves and coping when life gets confusing can leave us wondering if we're doing life right. In this case, I firmly believe you must judge for yourself. You decide what is the best way to express your version of beauty.

Is living *you* beautifully about sharing more intensity and passion? Are you expressing yourself best through pursuing some grand plan? Or, does living your relationships well express the finest you have to give? Maybe your peak expression is in a mix of all three.

Knowing what means the most to you offers pointers. By pursuing your passions, ask how you can contribute more of your true self. Consider, what greater good do you find inspiring? What kind of things have you done that left you feeling fulfilled?

Of course, understanding yourself isn't just about what you produce but also what you perceive. Your opinions construct your choices, which in turn feed back to your experience. Are you complicated? Yes. But in simple terms, we all evidence patterns in the way we interpret things. Discovering more about your own lets you identify the driving forces behind your thinking. Not only does that give you more control, it allows you greater fulfillment and protection.

For instance, becoming more conscious of your vulnerabilities is good insurance. Though we may not give it much thought, there are people and organizations only too willing to exploit us. Wanting to win us over, they mask their ugly intentions and prey on our weaknesses. Knowing your own vulnerabilities can protect you from cults, quacks, fads, and fraudsters.

Knowing more about what makes you tick is advantageous. But I believe the greatest benefit comes from learning to respect what you are personally capable of.

Desiring to be more of your beautiful self means treating your self as a resource. That might seem strange. But it's about recognizing your useful abilities as assets to be shared. Deliberately cultivating your talents to make them grow is part of that. Healthy self-awareness is about developing your ability and letting it flow out. Giving priority to those parts of yourself that you respect and having insight into the rest is empowering.

To me, self-knowledge is about nurturing the wellbeing of both yourself and those around you. It's about connecting the realities of your outer world with your inner beliefs to make life more satisfying.

Flexibility and a growing sense of awareness are also byproducts.

Being comfortable with yourself, you, along with your thoughtfulness, progress. More than reassuring, this newfound comfort lets you key into the meanings others are making.

By consciously choosing to live life on purpose, you can learn to stand tall being exactly who you are. By discovering your needs and drivers, you draw closer to purposes you can relate to. By finding more meaning, you not only find inspiration, but you will also draw closer to your happiness.

Finding Your Reason

Take a moment to reflect on how busy you are in your life. Now evaluate how important your activities are to you. How much feels satisfying?

Which tasks give you a feeling that *you matter*, inspiring you to take bolder steps? How much meaning are you able to make from what you've been doing up until now? On a scale of one to ten, grade how meaningful your life feels so far with ten being a life full of profound purpose and one being an utterly pointless existence. Give yourself time now to reflect on your answer.

With all the demands and possibilities of modern life, it's easy to feel confused. Just like the rise and dive of our confidence, so too can our self-knowing wax and wane. Whilst moments of excitement can paint a rosy picture, discontent has a way of feeding gnawing self-doubt. So I recommend you review these questions a few times over the next month to balance out the highs and lows mood states can bring.

Naturally, finding your personal meanings is not some little thing you do before getting dinner going. This is a process that can be as long or short as it takes for you. But a big chunk is taken up by simply getting your head around how pivotal purpose is in shaping the life you live.

Being unsure about what really matters to us means fulfillment feels elusive. Letting habitual life dictate our days, we can dodge thinking. But we can't avoid disappointment. Contentment can only come when we build our reason for being.

Despite many experts and leaders insisting they know what's best for us, you still need to think this out. Making sense of your life is bound to be personal, intimate, and, sometimes, confronting.

I believe nobody else can tell you what your individual purpose is. I know that will raise some hackles. But this kind of meaning is beyond persuading. Personal reason is about joining the dots on who we are and what our unique contribution can be. It needn't clash with other purposes. Just that each of us needs to be free to decide our own meaning for our own selves.

But the experience of living your life qualifies you with a unique knowing. This is your journey, after all. Discovering your purpose is part of living your worthy life, and this is something you know more about anyone else.

> *"Your work is to discover your world and then with all your heart give yourself to it."*
>
> Buddha

Purpose needn't be some mystical thing. You might find it cloaked beneath a variety of activities and seemingly separate events. So it's beneficial to start sifting through the things you do to find the signs.

Perhaps your cause is entwined in the purposes of others. Explore this further, but be prepared to stand apart, or even alone, if it means being true to yourself. Some people may resent you for being different, so be prepared to recognize it for what it is. Try to avoid taking people's controlling behavior personally.

Instead, remain open to the things that truly move you. Personal meaning need not be screamingly obvious or even especially attention grabbing. It can be subtle. Even deeply secret.

Though this will be challenging, finding your particular reason is doable. You are not embarking on a quest to understand the Universe. Just making your life count.

People all too easily go global whilst forgetting the personal. Wanting to know *"What is the meaning of life?"* they get stuck on the celestial questions, ignoring the tangible. But how much more powerful and exciting is it to ask, *"What's the most meaningful thing I can do with my life?"*

As I said, keep looking at the way you live for the clues given by your actions. As expressions of your values and beliefs, remember your actions reveal the meaning you're living right now. Most importantly, examine your conscious efforts. They deserve particular attention.

When you are doing things that matter most to you, you are living closer to your true purpose. Satisfaction rests on what we feel is our greatest contribution. It is therefore worth keeping our eyes open to our abilities and what we value.

Doing what you believe in is affirming, but suppose your beliefs don't inspire you. What then?

Though our certainties usually rise to the surface, it doesn't always mean we faithfully follow them. You can feel conflicted about your parenting, career, faith, and relationships. On top of that, decision-making can also be restrained by duty. Doing things out of obligation can oppress the rest of your beliefs.

Our financial burdens can also dictate terms, can't they? We might work in a job we constantly dream of escaping. Given most people are living somewhere within ten percent above or below their means, feeling trapped is an all-too-common experience. Whatever your income, you will always have to pay the bills. So how can you live your dream and still earn enough to live your life and find satisfaction?

> *"Most of us tend to live in one room most of the time, but unless we go into every room, every day, even if only to keep it aired, we are not a complete person."*
>
> Indian Proverb

For me, it's important to know dreaming of escape is not an end point. Nor is it a purpose in itself. Still, if it's a theme that keeps recurring, change of some kind needs to be applied.

Being caught between someone else's values and our own can result in a slow, simmering disappointment. After years of pretending to be something we're not, the answers to fulfillment are likely to be buried beneath an excess of mental baggage. Discovering your purpose, therefore, calls for fresh thinking and the willingness to be curious.

Firstly, where do you find inspiration? I suggest anything inspirational that keeps coming to mind shows signs of extra significance. Try writing down whatever motivates you.

Recurring visions that, for instance, make your heart skip a beat seem to come from deep within the self. The longer they keep reappearing, the more you should take them seriously. So if you have dreamed for years of being financially secure, isn't it time you really started planning?

Sometimes moments of revelation won't make much sense. Even so, roll them around your mind and muse on the possibilities. Seemingly silly ideas might even bear the seeds for undertakings both beautiful and satisfying. So keep your mind open.

Ask your closest friends what they think you value most. What do they see in you? Does their opinion match your self-opinion? What about your parents and siblings? What do they notice? There's no need to explain. Just start getting a feeling for what others see in you.

Be prepared to shrug off anything negative. Sometimes what comes out isn't what you want, but stay focused and stick to your mission of finding your purpose.

Finally, consider your childhood fantasies. What did you dream you would be doing? Are there any clues in what you were drawn to as a kid that reveal key themes in your thinking?

If you do all these things and nothing comes clear, be patient. Sometimes we block ourselves from finding things as if the timing isn't right. Become more attuned to your true values while molding your life around them. No matter what you uncover, you are already on your journey. When you give the best of what you believe in, the journey has begun.

This is beauty you can live. Your confidence and inspiration generate an energy others can sense. The more certainty you reflect, the greater the effect.

This is not to say that you will be constantly motivated. Meaningful living rests on the steadiness of your decision and effort. Not just on the height of your excitement.

Wholeheartedly deciding to do something because it's worthy and true to you puts meaning behind everything. Despite the satisfaction purposeful living brings, life can still be toil and hardship. Contented or not, you will always be tested. Repeatedly. Pressures and problems may leave you doubting yourself. Yet, these are all part of real life too.

Having reason to live purposefully gives you the drive to keep going. With big enough reasons, you can face repeated challenges confidently and overcome them. Rather than fear and circumstances, your desire draws you forward.

Needing a new professional for our rehabilitation consultancy years ago, Ruth and I were required to interview a short list of applicants. Coming back to the office to interview another candidate, I was completely focused on this task as a priority.

> *"We can discover this meaning in life in three different ways:*
> *(1) by doing a deed;*
> *(2) by experiencing a value; and*
> *(3) by suffering."*
> Victor Frankl

As I was about to turn into the driveway something struck me. Something big. Really big.

Looking up to my rear vision mirror, I saw a ten-ton truck barreling straight at me. Two seconds later I felt its massive force slam into the back of my car. Catapulted one hundred feet down the road, I thought, *"What a strange way to die."* Indeed, finding myself alive and intact in the wreckage amazed me.

Forcing myself out from the debris, my first instinct was to rush back to the truck and check that the driver was okay. As I opened his door breathlessly, he flinched, expecting abuse. Instead, I was happy to be alive and know he was fine too. Shaken, he kept repeating, *"I just didn't see you."* Reassuring him everything was okay, we exchanged details. Then, pushing the remains of my car to the roadside, I could feel shock taking hold. Trembling, I suddenly remembered why I was there and what I needed to do.

Regaining my composure, I dusted myself off and assumed my responsibilities. So, mere minutes after the accident, I was co-interviewing a young psychologist and left the circumstances of the crash for later.

If that's remarkable, consider when, as a parent, you awaken confused to the distressed cries of your youngest. Fighting sleep and disorientation, you remember what matters. So that moments later a child finds comfort in their parent. Despite what happened the day before and what is due in the morning, you put your own needs aside.

So you become a parent who just happens to be there when you are needed.

Meaning puts everything into perspective. For this reason, doing things with heartfelt commitment to your highest purposes makes your efforts happen with satisfaction.

Chapter 5

Releasing Your Happiness

"Beauty in things exists in the mind which contemplates them."
David Hume

Knowing your purpose in life gives you the keys to happiness. Releasing all that is beautiful in you opens the door.

In this chapter, we explore factors of pace, permission, adequacy, and approval. By freeing yourself up and recognizing the power of focus, you can express your best. Then, as you do, you can refresh yourself with play, giving your serious side well-needed rest.

Helping you make the best of your efforts, we explore rhythm, reminding us that we are, each of us, unique.

Then we explore obstacles to expressing your beauty, including manipulation and self-loathing.

Most importantly, the concepts of *adequacy* and *approval* unveil a different way of determining your self-worth. Both become the basis for feeling good and letting go of expectations that are beyond you.

Together they point toward the dramatic influence focus provides for releasing your power to produce happiness.

Finding Your Natural Rhythm

Have you noticed that you possess a certain pace? It reflects your basic view of life. Not the pace of speed limits, alarms, and timetables. But your own, inner beat.

For some, moving fast, talking fast, and thriving on haste is a part of their natural order. Others find themselves feeling most at home with a gentler rhythm. Moving and speaking steadily feels right to them.

Even if the pace of life is as ill fitting as a baby bootee on a basketball player, we do our best to fit in. Breathlessly rushing or moving with agonizing slowness, the pace of life is compelling. But, whenever we can, we love switching back to our own natural speed.

> *"Music and rhythm find their way into the secret places of the soul."*
>
> Plato

More than fluctuating energy levels, your natural rhythm forms the background beyond moments of calm and excitement. Having our own inbuilt tempo suggests some important considerations. Where do we find places to feel comfortable at our own speed? What about our relationships? Do we speed up or slow for the people we love, retreating at times to reset our rhythm?

I believe constantly operating against your instinctive pace is grueling. Perhaps it offers a clue to conflicts beyond our awareness.

Being a slower paced person, I find it harder to be in the moment if everything is happening all at once. Contrary to my internal cadence, my teen sons happily say, *"Hurry up and bring it on!"*

Planning for our natural rhythm means being more true to ourselves. After observing so many children in schools struggling to find their niche, I believe finding moments in the day when we can move to our own natural beat is releasing.

Kids keen to run, jump, and play struggle to sit for hours in the lethargy of classrooms. Just as easily, some students are left floundering when things get going.

Consider your pace when making decisions about jobs and vacations or tackling the thousand and one other things needing your attention. Feeling more at ease, you have a better chance of handling the circumstances.

You can also take into account the timing of others too. Who are the fast and leisurely movers in your family? What about in your working life and social circle? They also need room to find their natural rhythm.

By allowing people to operate at their inherent pace, immense frustration can be relieved. That's why I recommend observing for a while to find the natural pace of all the people you care about. Creating greater harmony at this barely discussed level might be your way of putting them at ease.

But don't say anything about it. Let's keep it a secret, okay?

Giving Yourself Permission

If you have a tendency for whipping yourself for all the things you haven't done or beating yourself up for your mistakes and imperfections, I want to tell you something. You are not playing fair.

If you can, imagine stepping away from yourself for a moment. See yourself as if you were an unbiased observer. Not critical. Just balanced. What comes through when you see yourself as another person? Do you sense someone putting huge pressure on her? Or do you pick up on strong elements of self cruelty?

If either is true, let me ask, does that really work for you? Are you getting what you want out of life through feeling guilty? Or is there something mixed up about the way you treat yourself or let others treat you?

> *"But' is a fence over which few leap."*
>
> German Proverb

Give yourself permission to be human. Allow yourself the opportunity to try and, at times, fail. Nobody is wonderful all the time. We all have our moments simply because life can be unspeakably rough at times. So why should we expect to sail through it all smiling? Nobody does, except when they're putting on a brave face.

True, your part of the world may well start falling apart if you stop giving one hundred percent, but you need to receive kindness and acceptance too. If you aren't getting it from anyone else, you have to bring that warm-heartedness into your *own* life.

Give out acceptance in generous dollops, much as you'd like it for yourself. At least by giving it away, you're making things more how you'd like them.

Compare that to waiting for some knight in shining armor to come through the door and sweep you off your feet. It's a delicious fantasy. But certainly not worth putting life on hold for.

Kindle the beauty you long to receive. Share it and let yourself be warmed by the kind of compassion you believe in. Treat yourself. Not so much with ice cream and chocolate (my favorite vices too), but with self-nurture. By our choices we each are capable of treating ourselves respectfully or with critical cruelty. If you've had a lifetime of internalized self-abuse, it's time to introduce a new, stronger voice. No need to silence the critical words. Just question them with *honesty, wisdom, release*, and *heart*. Giving yourself wise and kindly self-talk brings the power of beauty into your inner thoughts. Immediately, there comes the possibility of seeing yourself with a kinder eye.

Rubbing your face into every bit of dirt, by contrast, is never going to help you live a beautiful life. So start a better way today. Think of someone, pick me if you're stuck, to be your encourager in your internal discourse.

The experts call this self-talk *psycholinguistics*, meaning the language of the mind. Happening faster than we can speak aloud, it is a forceful agent for shaping your thoughts and actions.

Given people frequently say their inner voice or voices are negative, a positive, reasoned voice deserves to be heard. Dare to ask different questions. Instead of asking if things will get worse, consider how they might improve. Ask yourself where your self-blaming thoughts originate. Explore your mind.

Integrate a reassuring voice into the conversations you have with yourself from now on. Tune in to your inner conversations whenever you can. Then give this voice airplay too. So next time you become aware of your self-deprecation, insist on asking your encourager what they think.

By adding a kinder, more reassuring voice, you bring a little balance to the barrage of self-criticism. This is imperative to living a more beautiful life. Otherwise, chewing yourself out before you've had the chance to succeed will forever keep holding you back.

Giving yourself the authority to challenge your critical self-talk, therefore, is a decisive step. With *fortitude*, it can be the beginning of much healing, both for yourself and for the people in your past. Therefore: Start *revering* the beauty in you. It's high time to make it happen.

Manipulating Me

Feeling controlled is an uncomfortable experience, isn't it? Be it in our families, friendships, or workplaces, we know the game of people-maneuvering has few rules and scarce fairness.

> *"The tongue like a sharp knife kills without drawing blood."*
> Buddha

At various times we also become the key players, taking our turn at steering people our way.

Often revealed in facial expressions and tone of voice, manipulation regularly relies on a certain code or meta-language to get the point across.

"Did you mean to wear that?" could mean *"Yuck! You look bad. Why don't you dress more like I do, so you'll look nice?"*

"You never call..." meaning *"You're not trying hard enough to love me."*

"What's wrong?" "Nothing" often translates to *"If you really cared about me you'd know. Unless you keep asking and showing that you care, I'm not talking."*

Do any of these sound familiar to you? There are umpteen expressions that we use in a variety of coded ways to make a point. *"I'm going to bed," "That's interesting,"* and *"We ought to do lunch"* are everyday examples. Naturally, we get away with them because occasionally they do mean precisely what they say. This gives them useful controlling power without looking obviously bossy.

The power of getting others to conform, feel guilty, or obliged makes meta-language a popular device. Putting a veil of social acceptability over our intentions keeps it under the radar. But by skirting a more honest approach, manipulative behavior can become ugly. Deceiving inevitably carries hidden agendas often tied to selfishness and indifference

So how do we handle meta-language when we hear it? From my experience, by being prepared to be straight in your dealings with manipulative people, you can combat their calculating ways. Probably they will deny it. But by speaking it up you reduce its influence and weaken its power.

If someone is trying to manipulate you, try speaking up the truth of the situation. This leaves manipulators less room to wrest control. Forced to work harder to wangle through facts, they end up having to play catch-up. Speaking with *honesty* puts you in charge.

One of my favorite ways of dealing with someone using loaded comments is to restate and qualify with questions. For instance, *"When you said 'I was only trying to help' did you really mean that you wanted to find out what they were doing? Is that because you're at a loose end right now and feeling bored?"* Restating proves we're listening and also allows us to address the problem more directly. If our understanding is off the mark, then this sidesteps any manipulative behaviors by gently getting to the point.

In my own life, my mother's main technique for controlling was mostly through manipulation. One by one, as we each grew up and left home, Mama fell to inventing spiteful stories. Criticizing us behind our backs for our supposed nastiness, she would try whipping up a reaction, pitting us siblings against each other.

When we became wise enough to understand what was happening, none of us bought into her stories anymore. If she started telling me how cruel my brother was, I would put my hand up and say, *"You can stop now. I'm not interested. Tell me about something else that's important."*

At first, Mama was flustered and indignant. However, she soon learnt to accept it. Though it never fully stopped her trying, she must have realized criticism and lies were losing their firepower.

Like Mama, some manipulative bosses employ similar techniques. Instead of inspiring, they typically use meta-language for pressuring, threatening, and overpowering.

Awareness and a stronger sense of self are top priorities to cope with this sort of thing. Together, they give you a foundation to handle manipulating behavior. On this basis you can have the courage to speak the truth and the *wisdom* to do it well.

But what about ourselves? How do we reduce our tendency to talk in code for the sake of garnering control? The first step is becoming conscious of your communication. How much do you manipulate others? Who do you choose to use and in what ways?

Think about what you really want in these situations, and speak plainly. If the matter is about your feelings or opinions, try building your comments around *I feel* statements. For instance, *"I feel hurt when you start mimicking me"* instead of *"Do you always have to do that weird mimicking thing, you creep?"*

> **"Happiness is when what you think, what you say, and what you do are in harmony."**
> Mahatma Gandhi

Frequently these patterns of communicating are repeated through force of habit. So using ways to speak with kind directness, rather than coded signals, could feel strange at first.

Saying *"Dear, could you please take the trash out?"* instead of *"That trash looks full…"*; *"Have you thought about the trash?"*; *"I'm sick and tired of doing the trash!"*; or *"I wish there was someone thoughtful enough to take the out the trash"* reduces the risk of emotional explosions.

Clearly saying what we'd like to have happen also removes any confusion. Either way, the trash might still stay put. But at least you're making yourself clear in a way that is neither confronting nor manipulative. Directing attention to needs rather than creating issues also protects our relationships.

Now this is a truly huge area to explore and we're only just touching the sides. After all, sending coded messages is deeply embedded in our language and culture. For this reason, consider changing the way we speak a work in progress. I recommend starting with things that you routinely talk about in daily life and progressing from there.

It can be subtle or significant, but speaking with respectful honesty is a beautiful habit to cultivate. Adopting it elevates the listener and puts dignity in your expression. In turn you support a stronger sense of your own significance: a crucial measure in overcoming the struggle for self-acceptance.

Sidestepping Self-loathing

Have you noticed that feeling good about yourself is difficult to keep going?

Chopping and changing with the mood we're in, we can easily switch to feeling inadequate and disapproving. But despite the fact we sometimes feel this way, we keep thinking we're alone in this. That person you know with unflinching confidence? You can be assured that in their private moments they're not feeling super adequate either. Just as some people have fewer feelings of inferiority, others are naturally better at appearances than others. But no one fully escapes. There are times when even great leaders dread the limelight, hoping people don't see through their blustering facade.

Feeling inadequate is one of those awkward realities we selectively accept. Fine for some, but not for those we heavily rely on.

Depending on people for our own ends, we expect stability. For the same reasons, you can also be sure people want to believe in you too. They want to rely on what they value in you.

So what is adequacy after all? Better yet, how do you get an extra helping?

Since having children of our own, I discovered how much I love babies. Becoming a parent with our first-born changed everything. Overnight, babies stopped being noisy, peeing, and pooping things. Instead, they transformed into the cutest, most adorable people of all.

So whenever I find myself gazing happily at someone's baby, I am reminded of a powerful truth: how we *perceive* value molds our appreciation.

When babies are born, they all come into this world adequate. Like a tiny kitten or puppy, we too arrive as wholly adequate human beings. Having been defined by our birth, nothing more needs being added.

The trouble comes as we grow up. We begin doubting whether we are good enough. Most often, the rest of the equation is *"...compared to someone else who we think is better."*

Now believing your value as a human being is inbuilt from the day you were born. I'm going to add a bit extra. Coming into this world as babies, I believe we are all of equal value.

You might say, *"Well that's not true, Christian. A rich family's baby is more valuable than a poor one."* But aren't all babies precious? Whether born to humble or wealthy surroundings, all babies have a certain worth that inherently comes from being a child. Whether or not they are loved and cherished is not the measure. *Adequacy* is our birthright.

Now we can all experience feeling more or less adequate at different times. But I prefer giving this another name. I call this *approval*, and it comes from both ourselves and others. Changing with situations and emotions at any given moment, *approval* is fixed to our thinking.

Though becoming separated from your sense of *adequacy* is common, it's still there. Your *adequacy* remains lifelong as the bedrock of your being. Whatever you do or don't do, your *adequacy* is permanently tied to your humanity. You cannot erase nor increase it. Resting beneath thinking and doing, you are adequate whether you know it or not.

That's the problem of course. Most of us *don't* know it. Confusing approval with *adequacy*, we question whether we are deserving or unworthy. Congratulating or condemning ourselves, we pit our identity against others' and judge them all. In this jostling for recognition, we are constantly rating ourselves over the way we look, think, and act.

Mixing up these two beliefs is, I believe, the cause of untold despair. Knowing the difference between *adequacy* and *approval* is therefore vitally important. Realizing you are adequate not only gives you a firm footing, it also gives us a shared dignity. You and I need both if we want to sidestep the ill effects of inadequacy and self-loathing.

If protecting your self-worth matters, then picturing *adequacy* as separate from *approval* has an insulating effect. Regardless of what anyone says or does, your *adequacy* is not a subject of judgment. It remains a property of your existence, indelibly anchored to your humanity.

Recognizing that *approval* dominates our attentions but deals with an outer layer puts it into perspective. In doing good deeds, we can create things of merit, achieve higher status, and build self-confidence. Our accomplishments can also lead to us gaining greater popularity and respect. That can set our self-approval soaring, but it cannot enlarge our *adequacy*.

Likewise, we may struggle to achieve, repeatedly failing and finding social disapproval. Our self-approval rating could understandably take a dive. Yet, despite this, our *adequacy* remains beyond question.

Of course we are infinitely more complicated than that, aren't we? Perceiving has a way of shaping unrealistic positives and negatives too. No matter how much *approval* comes our way from others, we block or amplify it depending on how we feel about ourselves at the time.

How comfortable we are with ourselves is a controlling factor. If we intensely disapprove of ourselves, we can begin believing in our own inadequacy. Feeling unlovely and ugly can dominate our sense of reality. Believing we are becoming what we feel takes us into self-destruct mode. Being dealt a cruel hand and experiencing a lousy upbringing can get us believing we deserve little and will amount to even less. But we are born fully *adequate* humans, and nothing can ever change that.

At some stage I imagine you, like everybody else, have been subject to criticism and shaming over your appearance. Despairing, you may feel you have failed in some way. Our ideal self may be so far from our true self that we are left feeling totally inadequate. What then? Understandably, our *approval* takes a battering. Yet the intensity of

> *"Without forgiveness, there's no future."*
>
> Desmond Tutu

our feelings has no bearing on our *adequacy*. At our worst we remain an *adequate* person with low self-approval.

Clearly, *approval* is important for our general well being. But its notoriously fickle nature presents many problems.

One of the best things you can do is to affirm yourself with constructive action. This is important because it can do such great things for your self-approval. If we believe our approval deserves to rise according to our efforts, then positive action is *the* solution. Creating beauty helps faltering self-approval levels far more than nice affirmations. Changing what we can for the better and learning to accept the rest puts the power in our hands. Where it rightly belongs.

But, again, there is something crucial to remember. However beautiful your achievements are, they are a measure of your handiwork, not your worth. Though your self-approval will wax and wane with your triumphs and failures, your *adequacy* is never in question. You cannot add to your self-worth with things or achievements. Nor can anyone take it away from you.

> *"The promises of this world are, for the most part, vain phantoms; and to confide in one's self, and become something of worth and value is the best and safest course."*
>
> Michelangelo

I believe we live life best by basing our *adequacy* on simply being and building on that. Then, using our actions and intentions, we can set out to weave a satisfying life. Your actions are your hallmark. But their value comes from you.

Freeing Up

Releasing yourself from the torment of never feeling good enough is just a part of freeing yourself from a host of overwhelming burdens.

So whilst screaming is definitely an attention-getter and pressure release, letting go is better still. When we're so busy fighting life's spot fires, where is the time to do everything that's needed? Much less to do anything *we* want to do?

Consider that last night's argument is still leaving you smarting. Apologies have been made, but there's no eye contact yet. There's a whole day ahead, but you're not ready.

In the kitchen, putting things away, something spills. Now your clothes are a mess. You're running late as it is. But what about the kids? They're not even dressed, and everything is still in the wash.

There's been a breakdown too. Not you, but an appliance. So now you're in charge of chasing up repairs. Then there's also that problem at work that needs fixing. Which reminds you, what about that gift you've been meaning to get for your sister? But what to get her? She already has everything.

Now the phone starts ringing, the cat starts scratching, and your son starts yelling for socks from his room. For some unknown reason, you're starting to sound, and even feel, a bit brittle. Your mother is on the line wanting a long chat, but you fob her off. Just another thing to explain later and feel guilty about now.

And so it goes on. Not every day. But when you're feeling too overwhelmed to do justice to it all, there's only one thing to do: be prepared to let some things go.

Saying it is simple. But, as you know, the difficulty is in the doing. If you like getting things done and following through, letting anything slip feels like a personal loss. Not doing what we feel we should do can feel like failure.

My advice? Let it go anyway. If only for a while. Only choose the matter of life and death things. Then manage them well. Shrug your shoulders about the rest for now. More than likely you will come back to them later. Or perhaps they won't even matter when *later* finally dawns.

Apply wisdom to taking on and letting go. Practice the art of doing a few things well rather than multitasking in stressed out anxiety. Even if life has to be simpler to do it, only choose your top priorities.

You matter more than all the stuff anyway, right? So how come the stuff keeps taking first priority? Where does it say, *"Having grown up thou shalt be the slave to everyone else's stuff?"* I'm being cheeky, I know, but there's no point in people nodding gravely at your funeral, saying, *"Well we told her it would kill her one day. She was always one for overdoing things. Mind you, you have to admire her. She had the cleanest bench tops and never lost a sock."*

Instead, give yourself space to feel human. That means time somewhere, somehow without pressure. Living in a continual whirl can sometimes be exciting and make you feel important. But gradually, the adrenalin addiction gives way to an awful weariness. Sleep won't touch it, and no amount of makeup hides it. It is the inner fatigue of feeling spent, and it robs you of your sense of identity.

Being too tired to live, we drag ourselves out of bed. Then, with effort, we push ourselves through the demands of a day, finally crawling back into bed that night. This is life with all the trimmings. It looks great. But behind the curtain it's much less about life and much more about existence. Having the burden of umpteen things to do pushes us over a threshold. To a state where heartfelt life is swept aside and numbness kicks in.

We say, *"Wouldn't it be nice stealing away from it all?"* Just escape and enjoy the delicious freedom of being far from responsibilities. With a bit of luck, we might take a vacation and do just that. For a little while.

But the problem with trips is they're too temporary. You don't just *want* more time out; you probably *need* more. As much as you can create it, you need a life worth living in. Daily. Not a life you long to run away from. But a life in which you can feel wholeheartedly at home.

Of course if you live in a prison, *everywhere else* would be releasing. Your waking moments would cling onto future hopes for freedom. Yet even minus the crime, I suspect many of us are living like we're doing time. Freedom, forever on the far horizon, remains out there. Never here.

Which is why we need to simplify. Reducing the clamor and giving time to ourselves as we can.

Just to let go.

Matter of Focus

Does cutting down the demands do it all? Will it make you happy? How do I make life beautiful when it most definitely isn't? Fortunately, it is in your power.

There's something about you that's dangerous and delightful. You may not think about it much, but one of your greatest powers is the ability you have to center your attention. With it, you have the capacity to create beautiful harmony or utter havoc. The key is in choosing where your eyes rest and your feelings linger.

> *"Our life always expresses the result of our dominant thoughts."*
>
> Soren Kierkegaard

While seeking beauty we find it all over. Hunt for ugliness and everything supposedly good gets in the way. That's why we need to be careful where we point our thoughts. It might seem extreme, but your focus is like a laser beam. Directing it takes charge of a mighty force.

Think about selfishness and generosity. Both arise from our focus on them. Randomly or purposefully, with time, we gradually begin to become our thoughts.

When, as a kid, I was wrapped up in thoughts of free cash and candy, my kid-sized focus was latched onto getting. I had yet to learn that, whatever our age or ability, giving is the thing that brings the deepest satisfaction.

My attention to pleasure determined the measure of my contentment. Being caught up in wanting became all I could see.

To me, growing out of that stage is the surest sign of real *wisdom*. Not that we stop wanting things or ignore the pleasures of life, but we learn they bring little in the way of true fulfillment. Growing up, in the realest sense, happens when letting go of our wants becomes as easy as picking them up. Being less distracted, our focus is freed for deeper things.

This process is about intelligently evolving. Maturing, to me, is about deliberately using everything you've learned to make life worthwhile.

With something as potent as our laser-like focus, mastering its direction gives us phenomenal power. This is not a hard thing to grasp. Yet few understand it, and fewer cultivate it.

Whilst we do the focusing, it does the shaping. Whether shaped into becoming what others want us to be, what we think we're worth, or daring to be more than we seem, our attention leads us to a universe of possibilities of our own devising. Some splendid. Others disastrous.

To make your focus work for you we do need to choose. Hating and harsh judging are examples of choices driven by ugliness and unresolved feelings. In contrast, considered choice is the ultimate driver. Not under the influence of *oughts* and *shoulds* (which don't work properly anyway). But in deciding what really matters, we achieve the greatest opportunities for fulfillment.

> *"To be what we are, and to become what we are capable of becoming, is the only end of life."*
> Robert Louis Stevenson

Just focusing on bringing beauty to life is a thought-nourishing action. But by concentrating on beauty we create something vastly more satisfying. A life focused with purpose.

Seriously You Should Play

What should every stressed-up person be doing? The answer lies in going out to play! I'm serious about being silly. We should all be putting a value on playfulness, no matter who we are.

There's no need to be too serious all the time. In fact you can consider it a sign of poor time management. Making time for play or mixing it into the things you do is the tonic most of us are missing. Instead of downing a daily cocktail of peak-health horse pills and *trying* to feel better, charge around the house howling like a hound. Try it with a balloon stuffed down your top and your toe-tickling fingers at the ready. Or sitting down to breakfast together, and switching hands to eat. Alternatively, you could just rearrange your food to look like a smiley face.

Silly? Absolutely. Healthy? You bet.

If things are too solemn for that, it's time to create a new culture. One where everyone is allowed to play.

Consider the extremely serious soul. You know the type. Super uptight, with a clenched jaw and that *"I just sucked a lemon"* expression. Having shattered the gauge on their stress meter, they have forgotten how to be playful.

These people kind of look funny, but they don't need judging. They just need some good role modeling to see how it's done.

> **"How soon 'not now' becomes never."**
>
> Martin Luther

So what do I mean by playful? Well, nothing too expensive or structured is needed. Just more off-the-cuff messing around. It might look like nothing, but beneath there's plenty happening between a giggle and a chase. Play bonds us together, keeps our mind younger and fresh, and lets us off the hook of being way too grown up for our own good.

My hunch is you know this already. Most people do. But life takes us down *Serious Lane* where everyone practices looking solemn, hoping others will respect us more. To me, this is a major shame.

When we're constantly in role, the joy of life is dismissed as pointless or immature. Whilst taking our work seriously is generally useful, we don't need to carry it through 24/7. Without playfulness to bring out our best, we have a lot of happiness to lose.

That's why, ironically, lightheartedness has a serious place in life. Encouraging novelty, playfulness breaks us out of the restrictions of a rut. By encouraging variation and variety, it removes the boredom of routines. Seeing things afresh minus frown lines not only feels good, but it encourages creativity. Call it *innovation,* and even the world's top CEOs start taking notice.

Being silly and having a laugh is so underrated. Yet we all know how good it feels to get together with cackling friends for a laugh and forget our cares. Hearty laughter brings the restoring lightness needed to combat the burdens in our lives we'd rather not reveal. Even daunting decisions somehow feel easier thanks to the freeing effects of play.

Enjoying good-natured mischief is a secret that loyal lovers know too. Together they share a secret realm where accepting possibility and fun feeds their lasting affections.

> *"Whoever is happy will make others happy, too."*
> Mark Twain

With room to relax and disclose ourselves, playing becomes a bridge between us and the world. Bringing our relationships closer, simple playfulness can cast a beautiful light on even the dreariest moments.

Playfulness is so therapeutic that its benefits permeate everything. Bringing day-to-day cares down to manageable size, play is the perfect tool for releasing frustration and tension.

So when you're up to your neck in things and you've had enough, try these to loosen up a little. Decide to only take yourself half as seriously as you normally do. If play doesn't come naturally, try pretending you're a kid again. After all, we're all just kids with years on us, aren't we? Grasping life from a child's sense of things switches interpretation off and experience on. It allows you to sense things anew. As a bonus, you get some headspace back, letting you rediscover the simplicity of things you otherwise can't see.

To take it another step, you can try eating something kids eat. Pretend you're a kid by freeing yourself up and physically moving the way they do.

When our boys were little, I developed various flying scenarios to assist with helping them eat their all-important greens. Getting control tower clearance, cargo plane spoonfuls took off from their plate before circling, ready to swoop and dive into a willing mouth. Occasionally overloaded spoonfuls would crash, or detour elsewhere around the room with me in hot pursuit, providing commentary.

As a rule of thumb, if it makes you feel silly, you're on the right track.

Watch the way children and pets play. They aren't aware of what anyone thinks. They're too busy living in the moment, wrapped up in whatever captures their interest most at each instant. Experiment by living an hour like that for a completely fresh understanding.

For a while, skip being so grown up and forget your responsibility wrinkles. Release your self-conscious, responsible side and have some fun with someone. For lasting results, practice daily (and stay off the horse pills).

Chapter 6

Building a Beautiful Life

"Only from the heart can you touch the sky."

Rumi

Harvesting Your Burdens

You may not know this, but you have a goldmine. Buried under the mountains of problems you have endured throughout your life, its wealth lies forgotten.

Many of us have problems we'd like to forget too. Perhaps we wish some of what we've gone through never happened. So we might prefer to forget it all. Or at least try putting it behind us. With too many unwanted memories, it's understandable. Aren't today's troubles enough to think about?

But amidst all the dirt and difficulty, there is treasure for the brave. Having struggled through the worst of your difficulties, you have known pain. But as a result, you have also discovered and grown as a person.

Pitted against your own set of personal challenges, you have been forced to find a way through a labyrinth of conflict. So, as difficult as they were, these challenges provide you with an incredible resource. Whatever you have overcome, you can now mine to extract value.

People around you need the kind of love that creates a safe harbor.

> *"Character cannot be developed in ease and quiet. Only through experience of trial and suffering can the soul be strengthened, vision cleared, ambition inspired, and success achieved."*
>
> Helen Keller

A person to talk to, feel safe with, and give approval. Gathering together your collected life wisdom from all your hurts and triumphs gives you that ability. Your understanding of pain can be mined for the insight and grace you need to relate to and nurture another.

With *vision*, every hardship and moment of suffering can be used for something good. Having grieved, you know from firsthand experience the hurt we can all experience. Though we each have our own unique problems, we can express tenderness of *heart* knowing, generally, it hits the mark.

Coming through difficult times gives you the potential to grow something precious. I call it *wise empathy or experienced kindness*. Surviving tough times refines your views. Putting their influence to use, if you choose, can turn your searing pain into burning compassion.

Ground and polished by all the hard things you've faced, you have facets that will reflect beauty brilliantly. If only you would reveal them. Wielding your beautiful strengths you can at least make your burdens serve you.

But what if lack leaves us feeling insecure? How do we go about giving what we don't have? If we're craving for love, can we give it to others? I believe the process starts with us feeling that need personally. Then, by reflecting, we can call up the mercies we've been shown. Knowing what they mean to us, we can then go on expressing our own.

Having your emotional skin deflated by loneliness, for instance, teaches you the virtue of kindness. Firstly for the comfort kindness gives you. Then for the gratitude you feel towards the person expressing it. Becoming sensitized through your hardship, you grasp and experience what tenderness means. Being lightened by the beauty of *heart*, you also want to pass it on.

We can all begin expressing beauty like that thanks to the kindness of others. Choosing, we can live the care we ourselves need. As a form of self-help, we can let our love and affection be the beauty in the lives of people we touch. Not driving us through desperation to win approval but reaching beyond our ordinary moments, pushing past our reserve of long-nursed hurts we'd rather keep secret.

I believe it comes down to this: you are most beautiful when you grab hold of your inner life and wield it as a blessing.

On either side of you now, people are carrying their own unique burdens and secret shames. With or without the words or awareness, you can expect they are missing approval and understanding. Nor are they being listened to enough. Most likely hiding their hurts deep under wraps, they wear a mask of control. These things are camouflaged, kept hidden save the telltale signs of stance and the look in their eyes.

Hiding emotional experience may be a practiced art. But if you're looking, you'll see it.

Eventually, the feelings we hold become part of our face. So that gradually our expression starts revealing its story. Take a long look at faces, and you'll see their stories of inheritance, life lived, and longings unmet.

Knowing hurt we can read it in each other. We can dare to reach out, giving what we ourselves may have long been denied. With direct understanding, we can recognize people's fears with the boldness that comes from knowing their pain. We are all unique yet very much the same. Needing to be needed and wanting to be loved.

Building a beautiful life means becoming what you value. By shaping and weaving it into something worth sharing, we learn that burdens are ingredients too. Nobody wants emotional pain. We want to run and hide from it. But by choosing we can make something beautiful out of life all the same. Gathering wisdom from the mistakes of the past. Finding reasons for forgiveness and the will for fresh starts.

Most of us find it challenging making sense of our problems. Some, having no meaning, feel too hard to accept. But armed with

> *"Who is the most sensible person? The one who finds what is to their own advantage in all that happens to them."*
>
> Johann Wolfgang von Goethe

this knowledge, we can offer a helping hand. With *wisdom* and tenderness, we can use our hurts, transforming them into something beautiful. Something revealing our worth.

Juggling Plates

By harvesting enough experience, we can deepen our sense of dignity. Through it we can find our poise.

As it stands, people search endlessly under the wrong rocks trying to find balance. When it comes to being busy there will *never* be enough hours in the day. Ever. Despite the sway of business thinking in our personal life, achieving personal balance doesn't work in schedules. You can't slot your kids in at four o'clock for forty-five minutes. Then fit your mother in for fifteen minutes at quarter till five before getting dinner fixed, eaten, and cleared away. After which, scheduling forty-nine minutes to slip into something glamorous as you casually sip drinks with your partner, settle the kids, tidy up, take a telemarketing call, put the dog out, and go to bed. Then do it all again the next day.

> *"Time is an illusion. Lunchtime doubly so."*
>
> Douglas Adams

Forget things like the twenty-three-second makeover, sixty-two-second scheduler, and super filing organizer that sorts your life out in seconds. They're lying. Real human beings with feelings, thoughts, and relationships don't live happily in strict modules of time. Nor can balance come from a tightly time-slotted diary. It's a complete myth.

For many a family with young kids, the time around dinner is the *arsenic hour.* Grumpy kids and weary parents go through the motions of mealtime with nerves fraying and missed mouthfuls straying. In between preparing, consoling, and cleaning, there are the unwanted phone calls, visitors, and the general din. Yes, there are appointments to keep and jobs to get to on time. But real life also happens *between* appointments.

That's not to say being organized isn't important. Planning helps you make the most of your time, doesn't it? Without it, you would be hard pressed to get nearly as much done. Besides being in a world of timetables, organization is a must have tool unless we live in a village or a tent in the Sahara.

But there is something more fundamental to a balanced life than an efficient schedule. That life goes deeper than our personal organizer can measure.

> *"Science is organized knowledge. Wisdom is organized life."*
> Immanuel Kant

For all the running around chores and multiple to-dos, we certainly need to keep our *whys* foremost. As I've said before, the more meaningful, the more worthwhile. Being equipped with purpose, we can at least face even the most trivial tasks with certainty. If they are worth doing, they deserve our commitment.

But that's not enough though, is it? Most of us have important things to do. Yet even with a reasonable schedule, things easily go haywire. Balance remains a fantasy. There just isn't enough time to attend to everyone else's needs, leaving yours unmet and unfulfilled.

Overworked, frustrated, and tired, demands are splintering our identity into different roles. Roles like parent, career person, partner, cleaner, home organizer, lover, friend, and taxi driver (to mention a few) become part of your position description. With countless demands on your hours and abilities, no wonder you ask *"Who am I in all this?"* and *"Where is the real me?"*

Having vital things to do ratchets things up. Knowing you urgently need to get things done offers purpose, but it robs you of any semblance of balance. When you're stressing over parking, joining an unbelievable queue, or putting up with stuff ups, purpose piles on the pressure. Unless we remember something that rarely appears on our radar. That to cope under pressure, we need a strong understanding of who we truly are.

Being aware that you are important is not some pretentious thing. Your significance matters mainly in the way you influence people around you. Thinking this way won't give you any extra daylight hours. Nor will it stop traffic jams, people being rude, or all the other nuisances that beset your day. What it will do is remind you that your actions have influence.

Someone goofed? How you handle what has happened makes all the difference. Just got a ticket? Rather than slanging off in a verbal attack or blaming yourself viciously, hold yourself high. When difficulties present themselves, balance the "theory" of a schedule and the purpose of your tasks with your own sense of dignity.

Regarding your worth more highly means being less inclined to blame when things don't go to plan. Facing problems and pressure with a strong sense of dignity changes the view. Instead of ricocheting in reaction, you allow yourself room to be calm and composed. Not gritting your teeth and looking daggers but conscious that your actions are your greatest statement.

Feeling obliged to pack a mountain of things into a day gets plenty done. But when we feel the lesser for it, something is wrong. Having that knowledge is like a meter warning you to pull back before you overload.

Certainly the notion that we each have a sense of dignity has commonly been forgotten. But if we want to live well, it's time we started claiming it back. It's time we start carrying ourselves with the knowledge that our words and deeds *do* matter. That simply by doing all the normal things, we touch the lives of others dramatically.

To reflect on this, let me ask you some questions:
- When you are busy, how well do you treat others?
- Beneath the pressure of real life, how well do you handle people's mistakes?
- What do you do when someone cuts you off, barges in, or otherwise ignores your presence?
- In a difficult situation, when have you surprised yourself with your graciousness?
- How civilly can you say no to doing things that overwhelm you?

Your practical responses to these circumstances give a glimpse of your identity in action.

Having personal honor motivates us to be mindful of our overall character. We have reason to engage in situations because we know we have influence. Knowing we matter helps us see how others matter too. Rudeness and demanding selfishness, in contrast, come when people forget who they are. Forgetting their sense of honor, they replace it with defensiveness or arrogance. Self-justifying, they treat people with ugly contempt. Widespread, this undignified behavior has swept across society like a pandemic.

Thankfully we can influence change. Displaying personal dignity can put balance back into every facet of life. Priorities, based on our noble values, cut through the noise of selfish demands. Dignity also affirms the realization that only having two hands is not an apology but a reality.

Having a greater sense of dignity in the bustle of life is the way of poise. An approach that evens productive activity with self-expression.

By contrast, balance in your hours is a forever-moving target. We will always be striving to find the time for things aside. It's part of a busy life.

That's why living fully in the reality of now, rather than waiting for free time, loosens you from the tyranny of not having enough hours in the day to be authentic. Balancing, for me, works best when I'm not just at it and organized, but when I am deliberately being myself.

Facing the Hard Facts of Life

Naturally, sugarcoating life's challenges does look appealing. But there's no denying life can be tough.

Within some schools there is a lot of sweet-talk going on. With good intentions people are frequently attempting to make struggling students feel better with vague praise. Teaching kids to repeat, *"I am special"* and *"I can change the world"* looks harmless enough. But when it's not linked to effort or something children can see to prove it, it's useless. At best, it's a feel good fling. At worst, it's deluding and confusing. *Special* compared to whom? Yes, changing the world is a great goal. But how about starting with schoolwork and getting recognized for that?

With nothing backing up these declarations, kids soon identify them as painfully lame and ludicrous. As truth diviners, kids do a pretty good job overall. As much as they love candy, kids don't want their life facts syruped over. They appreciate the unvarnished truth told at their level. *Honesty* is something they not only value, they need. Which is just what we as adults need too.

When people are hurting, telling them to feel happy only reinforces their misery. Knowing that they *ought* to feel better piles on yet another thing to feel bad about.

Praising needs to be tied to real actions that are praiseworthy. Anything less feels patronizing. Likewise, if the situation is bad, it's better being clear.

That's why I want to be direct with you now. Facing hard facts is rough, but it's infinitely better than denial. Facing up to our flaws and not pretending them away puts us in a position of strength. You have imperfections which you might hate. But then, don't we all? Accept them and concentrate on what you have to offer as a person.

Feeling compelled to be perfect keeps us trapped in a cycle of inadequacy. Forget it. You can *never* be good enough. To be fully approved of, one must be completely perfect. Even if it were possible, it would be a very alien place for any human.

As you connect with your ability to create and perceive things of beauty, I believe in meeting your weaknesses with neutral awareness. Rather than shading our fragilities with guilt, attentiveness becomes a helpful step toward gradually overcoming them.

> *"People grow through experience if they meet life honestly and courageously. This is how character is built."*
>
> Eleanor Roosevelt

Consciously begin looking for signs of denial in your life. Practice *honesty* with yourself over anything that you are trying to pretend isn't so. Try talking it over with someone wise.

The key to increasing your sense of presence is to boost your awareness of what presses your buttons. Deliberating spelling out your anxieties is not an exercise in reinforcing your weakness. It's an empowering process. For anyone wanting to experience a more beautiful life, I strongly recommend it.

To get you thinking, here's a list of commonly ignored life facts we all know. Calm comes in going from simply knowing them to fully accepting them.

- People will cheat you. They will lie and disappoint you.
- Sometimes you will fail.
- Most likely, you will know profound loneliness in your life.
- You will miss out.
- You won't always get what you want.
- At some point, you will feel deep loss.
- At times you will feel incredibly stupid.
- You will be rejected and ignored.
- Feeling unlovely, you will try all sorts of ways to escape from yourself.

Hoping somehow to avoid their pain, many of us deny at least some of these experiences. Yet these hard facts are common to us all.

By accepting that they are part of normal life we can:

1. Skip becoming victims. It's not us. It's life.
2. Interpret these things as we choose. With *The Seven Strengths*, you can even make something good come out of them.
3. Forget about blaming. Each is an opportunity to practice holding ourselves high, knowing that problems are just the stuff of life.

Beauty in the Making

How many moments are wasted in wishing? I used to wish a lot, hoping that somehow the mere act would make things happen the way I wanted.

> "There are only two ways to live your life. One is as though nothing is a miracle. The other is as though everything is a miracle."
>
> Albert Einstein

It didn't work.

Turning your beautiful thoughts into action where you are and with what you have is where the power is. By breaking through wishful thinking, you can accomplish far more than waiting for the right moment, the right conditions, or some sugar daddy's rescue.

The secret to creating beauty in your life right now is activated in the simplest of ways. It will give you the confidence and satisfaction to do more and keep on cultivating your beautiful habits. Creating and appreciating beauty are part of your nature.

Best of all, the more you keep doing, the more you find to do that enriches your life. Instead of hanging on for good things to happen, you can start making them happen yourself. Your relationships, your environment, and your view of yourself all await your transforming touch. Even the most ordinary moment is a canvas for your creativity. Not things to get through but opportunities to leave your handprint.

All recognizable qualities have beauty in them. Possessing enduring value they also bring contentment. Listening to people deeply with undivided attention. Respecting others for their life experience. Finding things to approve of in others. Doing things like this is life enhancing. So too is expressing great work habits, organizational ability, inspiring leadership, and reliability.

Most of us are prone to taking where we live and who we are for granted. But it doesn't matter where or who you are. Whether in the most prestigious and plush surroundings or the bleakest and brutal of places, you can begin growing beauty right here. There is unlimited scope for bringing beauty to life. By speaking kind words and sharing effort with gentle honesty, we can make beauty appear anywhere. Giving without strings and accepting others for the good we can see in them is as inspiring as it is reassuring. Such things matter because so many in this world feel unheard, uncared for, and coldly rejected.

Instead of *"faking it until you make it"* by forcing a positive attitude or trying to impress, the crux of beauty in action is your *desire* for it. Recognizing it and creating small moments of satisfaction in your daily life are the things that make the difference. Even understated, against a backdrop of discontent and ugliness, beauty draws and fascinates us.

> **"Give thanks for unknown blessings already on their way."**
> Native American Proverb

By actively searching out beauty and offering kindness, we are not only enhancing life, but we're less distracted by shabby thinking. Remember, you are not trying to be *"nice"* or impress people. Your awareness and desire to create beauty are building a beautiful life through the things you already do. So, by polishing your qualities, you can expect some of your beauty to rub off onto others too.

Just keep your focus on being the best of your real self. Doing so means your efforts become your calling card. Defining yourself with purpose and putting *The Seven Strengths* into action has the potential to reveal all that's beautiful in you.

Mind you, though your deeds may be pleasing to many, no doubt some will resent you no matter what you do. That's not surprising. So expect it to come. It's important to keep focusing on what matters most to you and tuning into beauty wherever you find it. Following the purposes of your own spirit and deliberately living according to the beauty you appreciate is a true pathway of happiness.

Decide on all the things you can do beautifully. Appreciate them by giving them your greatest attention. Whether through working or all your other interests, you can release limitless beauty with untold possibilities. You only need your awareness to find it and your character to release it.

Doing this is an exercise in finding your feet. A way of feeding your dreams and touching possibilities.

From everything I've learned I can say that a life lived well doesn't wait for wishes. You need to find your best as you see it and share it with the people around you. If you have a dream lifting your spirit, now is the time to share it with action.

> *"We are what we think. All that we are arises with our thoughts. With our thoughts, we make the world."*
>
> Buddha

Sharing Your Dreams

Don't be too surprised if someone else somewhere is finding inspiration in the same hopes you have. Despite our differences visions have many shared features.

Somewhere there are people already thinking on your wavelength. So follow your inspiration by seeking out people who share in your vision. Leveraging your abilities with like-minded people not only improves your prospects, but it gives you the pleasure of working together.

Like fruits that have their season, dreams have their time. By all means let them germinate and grow in your mind. But be fully prepared to seize the day by tending them with effort and enthusiasm.

Pessimistic thinking is toxic for dreams, resulting in them failing to thrive. So weed out anything in your outlook that could inhibit their growth. Likewise, protect your dreams from the disapproval and ignorance of others. By keeping your dreams close, you protect them during the fragile stages of germination.

Nourish your dreams with optimism a few times a day; drenching them with feeling as you envisage them coming to fruition. Regularly pour confidence into their achievement to boost their growth. Then occasionally, carefully clip them as they begin taking shape to suit the conditions.

Come harvest time, the most beautiful dreams produce satisfying fruits everyone can share. So if you have a noble passion, make pursuing it benefit others as well as yourself.

Coming from the deep conviction of your personal purpose, feeding your inspiration with action feeds and strengthens your resolve.

Meaning if you don't reach the height of your ambitions, your deeds will still have worth. What you gain in moving toward your goals is decided by how you perceive it. Stopping at blame for not attaining some milestone would rob any learning. Too easily, we could dismiss the value of effort and give up too easily. Beyond disappointed feelings we need to know that beautiful schemes develop our qualities on the way. Just as obstacles give us the opportunity to reframe our direction and measure our daring.

Having been refined by *The Seven Strengths,* we can be confident in our dreams, even if they've been derailed. Through these qualities, all our interaction, effort, and planning can establish a potential not even loss could possibly erase.

> **"Satisfaction lies in the effort, not in the attainment, full effort is full victory."**
> Mahatma Gandhi

With *vision* that legacy can be transformed into something else of virtue. But only if we are prepared to persevere. How many of us wistfully bury our failures, blotting out our experiences with shame? Thinking it was our only shot, we can end up surrendering to passive pessimism and let life go. But if our dreams are noble, no bid is ever lost. Failed attempts are only first attempts. Keeping the beauty of our inspiration close, we can be certain that stuff ups are just warm ups. Dreams that keep coming back to our consciousness deserve our attention, not fobbing off.

We give up far too easily on the things closest to our heart because of a lack of belief.

Long before the outcomes, our greatest difficulty comes in trusting ourselves. Doubting whether we are worthy enough. Wondering if our own purposes are worth reaching for.

Visionary dreams are exciting. But beautiful dreams are awe-inspiring. Finding them takes time and insight. Giving us a reason to grow, all dreams test our devotion in realizing them. Achievement is no certainty, but struggle is. Whether daring to dream or just trying to get by, we all have a stake in that.

Dreams may be exotic, but their roots are firmly embedded in the basics of today. Just like our ability to receive others and truly hear them, dreaming is a matter of turning the regular into the remarkable.

Rich Listening

> *"It always seems impossible until it's done."*
> Nelson Mandela

Listening to people is so ordinary we don't give it much thought. Yet really hearing someone is a profound act. To actively be listened to is such a grounding experience. It leaves you feeling accepted, validated, and sensing that you belong. Being clearly listened to is a beautiful encounter.

Like a deep, quenching draught, rich listening is refreshing. Reassuring as it is satisfying, the beauty of feeling completely respected fills our senses. True listening is validating.

Good interpersonal communication recognizes we are not sharing the same experience, but instead we are living in worlds apart. Though our worlds may be overlapping, our motivations and passions remain our own. Consciously reaching out from our world of self-driven needs and desires takes understanding. To relate, somehow we need to tailor our messages, translating them to reach the unique realms of others. Though we can never fully know their reality, good communicators make intelligent guesses.

Whilst imagining what someone else wants, our talk often fails to make its mark. Directives may get results if the listener is acting out of duty or being polite. But, in the same way orders deny intimacy, communication without open listening lacks closeness and humanity.

Knowing we are in different worlds of need underlines the importance of listening. Hearing well, as you know, is far more than gathering sounds or recognizing words. Most often, what passes for listening is merely waiting for the next pause to start talking again.

We used to grin when Mama and Papa would get going on a theme and start talking over each other. Getting more excited by their own ideas, they simply stopped listening and began talking louder and louder. Maybe, having rarely been listened to, they felt insisting on being heard was the only way anyone would take notice.

Active listening means paying complete attention. With our eyes, touch, sense of smell, *and* hearing. Taking it all in, we can then interpret.

Somewhere around this point is where the blocking happens. How can anyone, for instance, make sense of the views of another if they snap straight into judgment by default? It is better to observe for as long as possible, leaving any review about what has been said for later.

Personally, I often find this difficult and demanding. Really listening looks deceptively easy. But keeping an open mind about what we are being told and how it's said takes deliberate action. Paying attention *without* making your mind up requires practice and patience. So much so that even highly qualified professionals in counseling can make surprisingly poor listeners.

The problem stems from our rush to make sense of things. Jumping to conclusions may go awry, but it works well enough and frequently enough to establish habits. Besides, it's easier than actively listening. Especially when we think we already got the point five minutes ago. Collecting the meanings we expect, we hurriedly dismiss the rest as unimportant.

Staff members dealing with a lot of people are particularly prone to process people this way. Going through their patter, they expect certain responses. Say something different, and they're unlikely to hear you. Saying you're not well when asked how you are could just as well get a response like, *"That's nice."*

> **"Everybody wants to be somebody; nobody wants to grow."**
>
> Johann Wolfgang von Goethe

Becoming aware of this lockstep habit of staying tight in our own world is disquieting. How long can we live without really listening? Judging by experience, I'd say a whole lifetime.

So how do you become a good listener? There are countless opinions, and I'm sure you have your own.

Practice certainly builds this skill. But I am convinced that genuine care is the crucial X factor. For good listening to create intimacy, compassion needs to be in the listener's heart. Without it, the person talking can only be conscious of your heightened sense of attention. This has its place, for example, in circumstances like business dealings. Given the situation, you might prefer to keep your relationship at arm's length. But even then, care adds something to listening that we readily warm to.

So, although challenging, good listening has plenty of benefits.

Your partner and family will appreciate the intimacy good listening gives as it draws you closer together. Better listening at work has the power to naturally boost your standing. By paying attention, working well with others, and being open to opportunities, you get the respect that you give.

> *"Behavior is the mirror in which everyone shows their image."*
>
> Johann Wolfgang von Goethe

Poor quality listening, on the other hand, exacts a significant toll. Preventing understanding, building barriers, and causing untold confusion, poor listening leads to missed value. How many relationship problems could be averted if people started wholeheartedly listening to each other? Indifferent attention creates costly errors, missed appointments, accidents, and distress. Yet rarely does listening get the respect it deserves.

Witnessing the impact of listening in health, business, and education, I've noticed patterns keep repeating. When people are actively engaging:

- Things work more smoothly.
- Efficiency increases despite the extra time taken to listen.
- Misunderstandings reduce.
- People work more closely together.
- Morale increases.

These patterns make our rising levels of inattention seem so remarkable. Despite lost opportunities, wasted time, errors, tension, and confusion, how often is ineffective listening identified as the culprit?

Practically everyone, professionals included, habitually fail to listen enough. Instead, we *pretend* to listen, a skill learned and refined as children. Nodding, looking, and making the right noises, we do excellent listening impressions. We can even kid ourselves in the process, thinking we've actually heard well. But it's a sham.

Actively listening takes concentration, and we have so many distractions, don't we? Modern life is making it even harder to listen as we multi-task with music, texting, eating, and speaking. Not only that, but saying what's on our mind is often such a priority we half guess the answers. So how do we get past that?

For me, reminding myself of the beauty of listening helps me to focus on doing it more. There are some excellent books worth reading on technique. But know that good listening is more of an art than a science. Conversations are unique, so each discussion is like a story in itself, linked to other tales before it. Skills alone cannot absorb it all nor do your relationships justice.

Far more important than skilling is overcoming any emotional deafness, distractions, and inattention. With *heart* our listening can transmit care for others. With openness and patience to let silences fall, we allow more than words to be expressed.

> *"The greatest degree of inner tranquility comes from the development of love and compassion. The more we care for the happiness of others, the greater is our own sense of well-being."*
>
> Tenzin Gyatso (The Fourteenth Dalai Lama)

That's why hearing a whole account takes heart as well as head. Sensing the unspoken means you need to fully be there with another person. It is a gift of time and self.

To be heard for everything you want to say, but dare not for fear of offending. That is true approval. Which is why, wherever you are, receiving someone with rich listening is a gift more beautiful than words. In the act of receiving, we state who we are.

Heartfelt Hospitality

Let me ask you, who do you know with that happy knack of making you feel most at home? What is it about them that leaves you feeling so at ease?

Helping people to relax and feel comfortable is what good hospitality is all about. Many cultures still keep holding it in high esteem. Yet it seems modern life is unknowingly undermining this beautiful attribute too.

> *"This life is not for complaint, but for satisfaction."*
> Henry Thoreau

Described in similar terms in other Northern European cultures, the German term *gemütlichkeit (gehr-moot-lisch-kite)* is often thought to mean coziness and comfort. But it symbolizes much more than a cozy place and friendly atmosphere. *Gemütlichkeit* also conveys belonging, cheerfulness, and a climate of ease and acceptance. Where there is *gemütlichkeit*, you can feel completely at home. Welcoming you the moment you step through the threshold of homes and restaurants, *gemütlichkeit* can immediately be felt. Putting guests at ease is first priority. Providing warm, cozy surroundings and attention, the focus is on soothing your cares and helping you relax.

Being welcomed into comfortable surroundings where you can forget your problems is truly inviting, isn't it? Though it features strongly in hotel and restaurant advertising, I suspect we mostly don't experience that kind of welcome too often.

Nor do people have a sense that *gemütlichkeit* is something we can take with us. Though you probably know people who do just that. Together, in their company, it feels natural to be yourself.

Having a *gemütlich* spirit, means creating a haven for others wherever you are. By being gracious and hospitable in the moment, you allow people to feel relaxed and safe.

With fear and indifference being daily encounters, giving hospitality by tuning into people's needs is a basic expression of living beautifully.

Being *gemütlich* means putting people at ease is a priority, not a watch-checking inconvenience. In the warmth of your relationship, people feel accepted. Stress melts. In your presence they sense connection. Releasing their burdens they become a guest in your presence. Within your hospitable warmth, they can leave their cares at

> *"You cannot always have happiness, but you can always give happiness."*
>
> Author Unknown

the doorstep of your company. With you they feel it's safe to be real.

Gemütlich people actively create a climate of tranquility in their relationships. Focusing their wholehearted attention on others, they consciously prevent anything unpleasant or negative in their own behavior from burdening their guest. Listening actively, they only seek to warmly receive. Leaving out anything stressful, the *gemütlich* host discretely stays in the moment.

Does life allow us to constantly be *gemütlich*? Hardly. We have responsibilities to carry out, deadlines to follow, and matters to share that aren't exactly soothing.

But the benefits of giving *gemütlichkeit* priority at least sometimes are enormous. Being so well received in the moment, your friends may feel as if time stops in your presence. They may feel a sense of healing just by being heard so openly and received so kindly.

By expressing your beauty, you cease being average. Instead, your influence has a life-changing effect on the people you encounter. Not in some magical way, but by the refreshing beauty you keep expressing. You become an initiator of joy.

Whether in your home, car, or just your immediate space, you can create a place where people feel at home.

You've done this countless times before, of course. Merely by focusing on whomever you are with, it starts happening. By keeping their immediate needs for comfort and appreciation foremost, you can't help but be *gemütlich*. Naturally, the more you practice, the better you get at it. But isn't it amazing how few people are aware of the needs of others? Simple things like finding out whether they are comfortable are often overlooked. Are they hungry, thirsty, tired, cold, or hot? Handling this in a fuss free way whilst still keeping your attention on their presence may seem minor, but have you noticed how few are fluent in the language of appreciation?

You don't need a flashy house, car, or fancy anything. Quite the opposite. *Gemütlichkeit* isn't about splashing the cash or winning admiration. It's about *heart*! Prestigious things can actually push people away from us, as they may leave them feeling inadequate. Being yourself, without trying to impress or convince, is the best way of putting people at ease.

Being normal is more appealing than all the showiness that's supposed to make us more attractive. Considering the pressure put upon us to look impressive, isn't that ironic?

> *"May you have warmth in your igloo, oil in your lamp, and peace in your heart."*
>
> Eskimo Proverb

Treating people as friends rather than visitors in your home brings people into a more privileged position. Real friends see you more as you are. Dishes sitting by the sink and clothes lying on the chair aren't a source of shamefaced embarrassment. They are simply signs of life. Instead of hurriedly cleaning up to give the impression that you live an impressive, glitzy home life, let go a little. Permit people to get closer to seeing you without pretending. You might even ask them to give you a hand in the kitchen while you're at it.

People wanting to know us are happiest when we let our guard down. Meanwhile, people who only pretend to be in a relationship focus on showing off. They are the kind of people who find it alarming when they discover you aren't living to impress.

So consider it a filtering process. Why not start sorting out who really wants to know you by being yourself with them? You can always save the scrubbing and fussing for whenever real royalty decide to pay you a visit.

Doing this may feel strange at first. Like leaving your underwear on the kitchen table. You can feel vulnerable. But if you want to become more *gemütlich*, the best way is to persevere. To push through vanity and appearances.

Having had a stream of overseas students living with our family over the years, we know how important it is to make them people feel at home. That's when you discover simple things matter most. Things like taking the time to always greet and farewell show that you care. Getting everyone to take part in helping and taking an interest in their comfort shows they belong. We all need that sense of belonging.

From time to time, we have also invited people to stay in our home whilst we have been travelling. Some are close friends. Others, strangers. Friends of friends have enjoyed our hospitality though we've never met. Seeing how each has treated the opportunity has been revealing. Some have been wonderfully gracious in return and left a beautiful trail behind them. Others used the gift with total disregard, exploiting everything. A few left our home in a mess.

Whatever we do, the message we bring to life is the one we leave by our actions. We all reveal ourselves through the little things we do as part of each day. Expressing our maturity, they lay bare our thinking. With no secrets spared.

When I begrudge sharing or ignore the needs of others, I am declaring the meanness of my thoughts and my self. From this I know hospitality is, above all things, a celebration of beauty and connectedness.

Chapter 7

Living Beautifully

"When you have only two pennies left in the world, buy a loaf of bread with one, and a lily with the other."

Chinese proverb

Making the Most of It

Full of rote and routine, daily life is often considered mediocre. Not so much living as just a warm up for the weekend or some great vacation when we get to do what we really want.

To bounce back we stave off the boredom with kicks. Tiredness, meanwhile, overflows and drowns everything. The *"too early"* alarm goes off, signaling you must leave your comfy bed. Signifying it's time to do everything you have to do. Survive it, and as a reward you get to flop back down again that night. Job's done. Then sleep fast because tomorrow you must do it all over again.

Living life like this is not so much a rat race as it is an endurance test.

Where is the beauty in that?

Well it seems to get splashed before our eyes in an endless procession of advertising and must-have products. Each is a manufactured reason justifying why we should keep running on the consumerist treadmill.

With glamorous magazine models, bright store advertising, and endless TV promotions, we are beset by a dazzling display of false beauty. Presenting an endless message, they declare beautiful living belongs to pretty young things and the fabulously rich. You can have it too. But only if you buy, buy, buy!

Just keep slugging it out in the daily struggle of *ordinary* life, and who knows? Maybe you too could get lucky and have a beautiful life.

Why should we be made to think this kind of controlled existence is as good as it gets? There's something missing, and I believe most of us can sense it.

Mind you, with so much conditioning, claiming beauty as something personal seems strange. To declare it's your birthright is outrageous. How dare we? So, of course we doubt it's in us. Just as we doubt ourselves, thinking *"I am no beauty, so why should I delude myself that I have beauty to give?"*

> *"The little things you do are better than big things you only plan."*
> German Proverb

We don't need to delude ourselves. Far from it. Nor do we need to try to fit into someone else's version of loveliness. For, this time, *you* are the one deciding what's beautiful from *your* viewpoint. You choose what *you* want to make beautiful in *your* life. In the process, even the ordinary will start offering more richness.

Instead of just surviving each day, life is about discovering. Thinking about how we can make our passing moments matter.

Whether advising clients, taking a call, cleaning the bathroom, or dressing a child, every moment you have can become your opportunity to create something that matters; something beautiful. In your mind, through your words, and with your deeds.

Crazy? Maybe.

Life is not so much made of big events as an interwoven string of little moments. Together they add up to make a lifetime. Either disappointing and empty or wholehearted and satisfying, your life is yours to weave.

Naturally some will keep insisting the only true way to be beautiful is to own the outfits, drive the cars, live at that address, and splash the cash. Believing that is quite understandable. To a point.

You see, the moment anyone feels they can no longer make anything beautiful without the trappings of money and status, they've been had. Effectively their conviction is that they are nobodies. To be *somebody* they need prestige, and prestige can only come from having lots of things and lots of cash.

Not surprisingly, advertising works this theme hard. Buy *Brand X*, and you too will be sublime.

> "The more you know, the less you need."
>
> Aboriginal Saying (Attributed)

It's no secret that as long as people believe they're missing something, their dissatisfaction will keep them compulsively buying. The shopping experience, for all of its delights, relies on the fallacy that *getting* brings fulfillment.

But living a real life of beauty is different in every way. Firstly, it invites us to think for ourselves, which marketers find harder to handle. Having been groomed to believe *"If only I can get that next wonderful thing then my life will be beautiful,"* we are easy targets for exploitation. The meaning of marketing is robbing our own. Mostly, we are trained to buy, not think.

So if we believe in making the most of our life, there's a point of decision to reach. Do we let others decide what's beautiful for us and then spend our lifetime waiting for its versions to hit the shelves? Or do we discern beauty for ourselves, recognizing its qualities both in things and relationships? One is about being a dutiful consumer. The other about being a person with purpose.

> "What do we live for, if it is not to make life less difficult for each other?"
>
> George Eliot

I know it's not clear-cut. But falling into line and believing we have no beauty will always be self-defeating. Whereas, deciding daily to actively discover and create beauty puts influence into our own hands.

These are *our* choices.

Sometimes, I like to call myself a Happiness Advisor because I'm driven by a desire to help people bring out their best. I am convinced that to find your happiness you need to keep using your strengths to their fullest. Believing in your potential to build beauty with your life is just the beginning.

Living more beautifully puts the happiness back into your hands. Your amazing capacity for appreciating and expressing is what makes your relationships flourish and your identity attractive.

That's why age and budget cannot determine the richness of your existence. Like your possessions and achievements, they reveal something about you. But your mind is not tied to these things. You are above them.

Creating beautiful moments in infinite combinations is one of your gifts. By *visioning* things fresh and new or giving *heart* to a friend burdened by problems, you reveal this tremendous blessing. Your capacity to turn daily situations to beauty is unlimited. You, as you really are, have the extraordinary power of turning nothing much into something supremely special.

> **"The face tells the secret."**
> Yiddish Proverb

Even creating beauty for our own enjoyment has a flow on effect. The satisfaction of a hobby or the thrill of sport spill over in your enthusiasm, so you can't hold it back. Once your eyes start shining and your soul lifts, your delight, like laughter, becomes happily contagious.

Living on purpose means even the most trivial things can do double duty. Efforts somehow benefiting others can become gifts. Thankless tasks, like housework or running errands, can become offerings of love. When you are exhausted, cooking a weekday meal might feel like a supreme act of giving. Because, fundamentally, that is what it is. Making tasks much more than mindless chores comes when you have good reasons to do them.

Resenting tasks usually comes because of a lack of appreciation, weariness, and boredom. Countering these resilient feelings needs passionate reasons. That's why, when the purpose is strong enough, getting our hands dirty is no big deal. Things can be made worthy because you care to do them.

As a teen, Ruth did part time work as a scullery maid in a retirement village. Once, whilst preparing a meal for a bedridden resident named Mr. Jones, a nurse came into the kitchen. She announced Mr. Jones wouldn't be needing his meal as he had just died. Shocked by the sudden contrast of life and death, Ruth suddenly realized her preparations were pointless. All the care and countless tasks we do are meaningless unless they benefit somebody.

Then she started thinking about all the countless moments of effort that go into a lifetime. All the practical care of raising children, keeping a home, educating and making plans work. They only matter because we matter. We are the value behind every meal, tidy, wipe down, work back, and phone call that needs doing. That's why our actions count. Whatever we do matters if someone, somewhere, gets something good from our effort. Without this connection, actions mean nothing.

Doing the things you need to do with dignity, and sometimes delight, expresses beauty. Each beautiful effort stands for something far beyond what can be measured in status or dollars. Choosing to put something of yourself into all that you touch gives everything the value of you.

Much that we do, of course, will continue to go unnoticed. We cannot expect the world to stop and begin marveling at our efforts simply because we've changed. What matters is that your inner self, who always notices your performance and intentions, keeps reaffirming your self-approval. By stoking your confidence, it also nourishes your motivation.

That same approach can also be used to build up others as well.

Consider, for instance, how much you value being recognized for your efforts. Longing for recognition, we all appreciate it, don't we? If not loudly, then often. We want others to say we are doing well and deserve more. But instead of waiting to receive praise, we can take the lead. Choosing to be someone who actively gives praise for all that's worthy fills your relationships with graciousness.

Practiced enough, the power and pleasure of delivering praise is on par with the satisfaction of receiving it. Tying praise to things people do well sidesteps vacuous flattery. Just as speaking highly of others without seeking a response goes beyond niceties.

> *"Knowing is not enough — we must apply.*
>
> *Willing is not enough — we must do."*
>
> Johann Wolfgang von Goethe

This is but one simple human need amongst many that we long to have fulfilled. We know our yearnings. Some to the point of aching. Yet what we lack can also give us understanding. Turned outwards our longings give us a heightened awareness of how to meet the needs of others.

By *giving* and living out meaning, we take charge of our life. Claiming every moment for beautiful reasons, we don't need to wait for weekend escapes. Nor for a lottery-inspired hope that our bank balance will finally begin bulging.

Right Now Living

Just living in the moment is a powerful thing. If life continually exists for the future, we can end up living less of a life and more of a plan.

Similarly, if we are fixed on the past, enjoying now with all of its possibilities has to be skipped. When people prefer reliving the past, they end up denying the gift of today.

Continually zoning out into the reassuring ways of yesterday or the thrill of future possibilities is a form of pretending. Robbing us of the power to fully engage in the here-and-now, it implies avoidance. A way of running away without moving a step.

During the instant you are reading this, you are responding to the moment. You are here, thinking about these words, and deciding your feelings. This instant is the only time you can possibly influence. Yet we keep forgetting that these are the very things that make our life. Rushing through, avoiding, and generally denying them in search of better instants, we habitually miss our moments. Clocks show them going by. But how often is their passing scarcely felt?

Marcel Proust, the famous French writer, had a way of getting the most out of his moments. No matter what he was doing, he discovered each small instant could be a rich feast of experience. If only it could be captured with awareness.

By extracting the significant from the trivial he sought permanence in a world where things, people, ideas, and feelings seem short-lived.

Making meaning from the ordinary, Proust believed, was the key to living more fully. Revealing *"the truth of involuntary memory,"* he famously described how even the sight, smell, texture and taste of a little madeleine cake can trigger a flood of remembrances.

Separating inner time from chronological time, Proust declared *"An hour is not merely an hour! ...It is a vase filled with perfumes, sounds, places, and climates!"* For Proust it wasn't the framework of facts but the lingering flavor of life that is the *"priceless everything"* making each moment in time unique.

> **"To see a world in a grain of sand**
>
> **And a heaven in a wild flower,**
>
> **Hold infinity in the palm of your hand**
>
> **And eternity in an hour."**
>
> William Blake

Proust passionately believed how we spend our time is how we *"create ourselves."* Yet how many moments do we live through detached, unfocused minds? Waiting for something to happen. Or just numbing out.

Living richly in the minute has secondary benefits. By tasting the full flavor of that mouthful of sweet melting chocolate, we can clear our head of most everything else. Watching a fly crawl on a wall is hardly scintillating. But study it and see how it moves. This is the way of a child. Staring, without insisting on how things ought to be from experience, children see things as they are. Like the first moments of waking and seeing without knowing, they drink pure, unnamed experience.

Switching off from self-consciousness is a wonderful thing to do. Practice touching, seeing, smelling, tasting and hearing with total focus. Doing this for a minute or two, at least a few times a day, connects you to the moment. Crossing fully aware into your surroundings with wide eyes unlatches the gate to a world that's intoxicating in its intensity.

By seeing everything so often, we end up noticing next to nothing. So, as an exercise in awareness, try being blindfolded for thirty to forty minutes. Then open your eyes to take in everything. Soaking up the moment, everything becomes more intense, more vivid, more real.

By contrast, rushing through our minutes with the urgency of a man on a mission means we miss it all. Too easily, goals and expectations end up taking us to places far away from the here and now. Good goals, the very best of goals, allow for now. Just as they also allow for the mistakes we are bound to make.

Whoops!

Remember the last time you seriously messed up? Well, there are better ways of handling those moments. When our best efforts go wildly astray, it's easy to go into finger pointing. But what does it achieve? Perhaps with confusion reigning, blame is a vain attempt at gaining control.

Overwhelmed, dismayed, and disbelieving, we briefly begin questioning everything. If the problem rests with us, emotions like anger and humiliation jostle for prime spot.

Being overwhelmed we become immensely vulnerable. Within seconds we start caving in and cop the blame, or we go on the defensive. Success, at this point, quietly vanishes from the horizon.

Foundering at the foot of failure comes easily, especially when others are pointing an accusing finger. But when we ask what we can learn from it, the experience takes on a new meaning. Damage can sometimes be irreversible and the losses acute. But misunderstanding and failure are rarely final.

Just bear in mind that messing up always offers a charged decision point. We can either let it prove our inadequacy. Or, seeing mistakes as part of life's journey, we can learn and move on.

Most of us don't give ourselves that kind of leniency, preferring instead to beat ourselves up with guilt. That's why, during these times, it's comforting to have the support of a wise friend.

Having another perspective on things helps. But if you've spent a lifetime self-blaming, it's going to take time to create more beautiful ways. The good news is that failure need never be an end point. Fresh pathways always offer new beginnings.

Remember, you don't have to be perfect to live a full life. Times will happen when you put your foot in it or seriously undermine what you've been trying to do. We each make mistakes. Guaranteed. The crucial thing is that, once done, we go on with the most virtue we can muster.

Fortunately, many mistakes are soon shelved by others as the pressing events of today vie for attention.

Meaning, when your boss starts yelling at you over something, it's not an end point. Nor is that fight you had with your partner. If you're like me, your default setting is to translate these experiences into complete catastrophes. Gradually over the years, I've been learning to take a step back. Knowing my emotions are wonderful senses but not great leaders, I now question them. Doing this leaves me headspace to start wondering what I can learn. This works very well when I'm feeling myself. Not well at all when I'm exhausted.

So long as you're not too tired, I recommend trying this technique out for yourself. The secret is obviously not in the lessons learned but in changing the way you view mistakes. This is helpful because most of us seem to have dysfunctional ways of handling oversights.

Goofs, gaffes, and blunders are more than a reality. They are part of *the* reality. Choosing, we can pretend we never have them by hiding the wreckage they leave behind. Alternatively, we can develop better ways of managing the aftermath. So you goofed. Now what?

Working in business taught me a lot about mistakes and it changed my thinking completely. Far from dodging complaints, for instance, I find them not only helpful but a great opportunity.

Picture this. While shopping you buy a pair of jeans from a fashion store for a bit more than you wanted. But on getting home and doing the fashion parade you find the zip is faulty. Annoyed, you end up driving straight back to exchange them. Explaining to a different salesperson, you can tell she isn't going to budge. Feeling anger rising, you demand to see the manager.

Coming out, the manager hears your story and immediately starts apologizing. Then she reprimands the salesperson who says sorry too. Seconds later the manager replaces your jeans and goes one further by handing you a discount voucher for fifty percent off your next purchase.

How would you feel? I'd go from positively bristling to so grateful I'd almost be whistling.

That evening you tell your family and friends what happened and how pleased you feel. You and the store manager impress them. Some of them will feel like shopping there too.

Beneath the surface, what are such service and product complaints about? I believe they arise when experience comes in conflict with expectation.

When it comes to buying, we believe the seller should treat us fairly. When we are let down, it's so disappointing we typically tell others.

But if the seller then proves they are more than honest and trustworthy, something remarkable happens. Restoring our positive feelings, they usually take us further. Telling everyone we can about the turnaround, we feel a greater sense of connection. A seller who demonstrates that, when the chips are down, they actually do care builds trust. Not always of course. But often.

Mucking up provides important tests of confidence in all relationships. Strange as it seems, most mistakes are not the problem but the attention grabber. What matters more than anything is how we handle them. Blaming others or denying are poor choices liable to amplify tensions.

Accepting responsibility works because it gives everyone a sense of returning stability. But, on its own, that's rarely enough. Doing something more goes one further. Instead of just covering the error, it actively generates trust.

Imagine accidentally dropping a friend's fine china platter. You immediately apologize. Then, quietly, you make a point of replacing it. Perhaps you even add a little *"dropping dish gift"* as a way to show care.

> *"The past cannot be changed. The future is yet in your power."*
> Mary Pickford

In countless ways, the mistakes we make are unexpected opportunities to live beautifully in the moment. How we handle our day-to-day stuff ups and the blunders of others is the crucial thing. Being gracious expresses what real life beauty looks like. Not planned or strategized for getting good effect, grace is just a way of accepting our true position. Though making mistakes is human, none of us need ever by defined by them.

Next time there is an error causing some kind of conflict of belief, recognize the opportunities it gives. By building trust, digging for *wisdom,* and creating a fresh starting point, you can utilize your mistakes and make beauty happen.

Cold Feeling

Those same actions also come in handy when we're facing the unfriendliness of modern life. To me, so much of everyday living in big cities is filled with cheerless indifference. Even people who have worked together for years can be surprisingly detached and bereft of warmth. Care and kindness are achingly absent in a society that continuously accepts apathy as the standard.

In a world where people are continually moving and doing, meaning can feel fragmented. Life becomes confusing. Activity seems driven by ulterior, sometimes mean-spirited, motivations. Crowding in the rush, everyone looks self-absorbed.

Waiting together with thousands of others in traffic is a remote feeling. Done day after day, it can feel like we're blurring into some kind of soulless collective. Banked up in well-defined rows, we remain nameless and unrecognized.

Scan the crowd in a packed train or bus. Scan freeways jammed full of commuters. What do you see? People all traveling together but fundamentally alone. Staring emptily away from each other, everyone remains separate, isolated.

Without connection we retreat into ourselves. Placing our thoughts back to home, work, music, or anywhere else we can find meaning, we collectively withdraw, pulling away from interaction. In the absence of care, we tune out to life in the moment.

Compare that with the happiness that comes from applying *The Seven Strengths*. People patiently waiting in the face of delays. Kindness in giving someone a precious seat. Creativity in handling blocked goals to find better approaches. Forgiveness instead of the finger. Compassion shown to strangers. Calm dignity instead of cold distance. Sharing, instead of forcing through to be fastest or first.

City life is compounding the burdens of work with pressure. Feeling dissatisfied, people are jaded and cynical. Fighting through congestion to get to work then wishing they were home, people are trapped by circumstance. Invisible dividing lines bisect life. Between weekends of living and weekdays of duty.

Then, when duties take over our free time, all the good life gloss of possibility starts fading too. As fantasies of escape build up, happiness gives us the slip. Line by line, burden etches its way across our face. Hardened by stories we'd rather not tell, we assume a cold life of limited fulfillment and beauty denied.

I wonder if you feel these common burdens too. To me, they reveal why beauty is so compelling and liberating. Transforming the silence of ordinary struggle, it is beauty that brings comfort and release.

Thankfully, you have the capability and the reason to put warmth into your workday experience. At home, driving, queuing, and in a thousand other ways, you can dignify the ordinary.

Putting *The Seven Strengths* into daily life is precisely where they belong. In the common blandness of commuting, the checkout, and a thousand domestic routines. Think of everything in life that invites you to shut down. Right where it's needed, beauty belongs.

> *"Do good and don't worry to whom."*
>
> Mexican Proverb

Every situation we find ourselves in that is bereft of care or fueled by self-seeking needs our presence. We are the means by which courage and compassion speak. By gracing situations with our own warmth, values, and certainties, we become the difference in the world.

Thanks to you and people like you, it's already happening. Consider how so much of life relies on beauty already in the celebration of creativity, entertainment, and persistent discovery. We look for leadership, hoping for courage and *wisdom* and, sometimes, we find it. When we share stories in print and film of perseverance, compassion, and self-sacrifice. Their influence becomes part of our identity. Their power is also our own. In everyday life, you and I are the true bearers of beauty.

Care

With *heart,* it's obvious. People know soon enough if you care about them. Surrounded by a world of fake concern, its reassuring and inspiring influence remains undiminished.

Care based on dignifying others has an enduring quality. Considerate actions showing respect and well-developed mindfulness are admired. When witnessed, they lead us into thinking bigger.

Being drawn to it, people feel they know us when we care. Even the care-wary have to work hard to resist it. Discrediting it as schmaltzy, weak, or insincere, critics merely expose their own inadequacies. But whether trusted or in doubt, selflessly expressing care has clout.

This explains why impersonating it is so weak and devoid of warmth. Selfish motivations, fear, fraud, and control use care for concealment. Hassling and fussing disguised as care hide disquiet and disinterest to coerce and cajole. For gain, deceptive salespeople make a ruse of caring. We are, after all, their meal ticket. This is care as a facade. Lacking honesty, it subtly undermines itself.

So, despite every attempt to exploit it, controlling care ultimately fails.

As an expression of *heart*, caring is difficult to measure. Nor can it be forced. Like love, true caring is personal, intimate, and beyond the understanding of people who lack it.

Through years of exposure to counterfeit concern, I figure many of us develop sharp senses, looking for evidence that care comes with genuine intent. Perhaps because we comprehend its true value.

> *"Eyes that do not cry, do not see."*
> Swedish Proverb

Generously offering care clears much ill will and overcomes many hardships. Through it, tenderness can be known and even the humblest house can become a home. Care enough and whole communities can come together with a growing sense of goodwill.

With *heart* we can treat people from all walks with regard and respect. We can give consideration because it reflects who we are. What's more, it feeds positively into our own sense of happiness.

So, as much as you are able, take an interest in everyone you have dealings with, no matter their background. Nobody can be thoughtless and considerate at once, can they? That means the more caring we are, the greater our potential to understand each other. Whilst tolerance chooses to accept differences, care harnesses it, bringing us into closer relationship. Care *connects* us with difference.

You are likely to find more connection than you might expect as people start opening up. Relating to everyone in your social landscape expands your horizons. Caring more widely gives you a greater sense of belonging and ease.

To feel calm and take comfort in the pleasure of rest , there is no substitute for care.

Sleep Healing

Ah, sleep. That wonderful sensation of enjoying a good night's rest and waking refreshed. Like air and water, you need sleep. For clear thinking, stability, and a satisfying life, shut-eye is one of the essential ingredients.

But who gets enough? With late night distractions, technology, and busy schedules, the quality of our rest is being diminished.

Feeling like we can pack more into our day, we try burning the candle, top and tail. It works, but the benefits come at a price.

Rule of thumb: staying up late borrows from tomorrow to expend today. Doing this often puts us into permanent damage control. Frequently being overtired makes concentrating difficult. With less reserve for coping, life gets gritty and more things go wrong.

How about doing yourself a favor? As much as it is in your power, make it a habit to get a good night's sleep. The immediate rewards are clearer thinking, being freer to live in the moment, and enjoying a better quality of life.

All of this rubs salt into the tired eyes of anyone suffering chronic sleeplessness of course. Having a constant battle with wakeful exhaustion, they know how vital sleep is. Willing to try anything, they are forever caught in a state of catch up. Hoping for a good night's sleep, they routinely settle for disrupted dozing. Then, waking easily at the slightest sound, they lie awake ruminating about yesterday and the coming day.

The reason why I am promoting sleep is to raise its profile. Sleep healing is without parallel. Yet we ignore how potent its curative powers can be.

Assuming you could do with the benefits of better sleep, let's explore this theme. Unless you have severe insomnia, chances are changing a few things could make a big difference.

Working with many adults and children complaining of sleep trouble, I found *habits* were the chief culprit.

From what I can tell, anything that goes against our natural rhythms is likely to reduce the quality of our rest.

So here are some suggestions that could help you sleep better:

- Habits help or hinder, don't they? So create routines to signal when it's time to go to bed at your place.
- Avoid eating too late or drinking too many fluids, especially those with stimulants like caffeine (contained in cola, coffee, tea, and chocolate).

- Make your sleep time routine a process of winding down early so your body can get the message.
- Create an established rhythm by bedding down your home and getting your family settled around a set time.
- Switch off the cell phone and any other screen or sound technology an hour beforehand to reduce stimulus.
- Read a book in bed and bring the lights down low, using a bed lamp rather than any other bright lights.
- Let your bedroom be a place of relaxation and calm by reducing or getting rid of anything distracting. Start by eliminating labels and text. Then, if at all possible, keep the world out of your sanctuary by making it a TV-free zone.
- Make sure it's dark enough too. Bright lights and the sun shining in too early can rob you of deeper rest.

We are all different. So of course it's a matter of trying out what works best for you. Certainly lots of physical activity during the day and getting concerns off your chest well before bed are beneficial. Both can help in counteracting physical imbalances, increasing the prospect of you sleeping more deeply.

But sometimes it's easier saying than slumbering. Babies, for instance, have their own sleep schedule that might disagree with yours. So even resting plays a vital role too.

When Ruth and I had Dan, we were working in our consultancy and I was also studying. Like most new parents, the first three to six months offered a challenging insight into life without good sleep. During that time we relied on napping to keep us going. Resting every quiet moment we could (even dozing sitting up at the dinner table during meals), we managed. Just as everyone else does. You find a way when you have to, don't you?

Perhaps you could consider sleep as an investment in lifestyle. Doing so at least lifts its status, giving it a higher priority against all of your other pressing needs.

Personally, I'm a big fan of the humble catnap. Whether you call it resting, power napping, or nanny napping, having a short burst of sleep for around twenty minutes in the afternoon is a good refresher for many. Long held traditions like the *siesta*, *mittagspause*, *bhat-ghum*, and *wujiao* suggest the benefits of a little after-lunch rest have long been respected.

Grabbing a catnap, however, probably won't go down well if you're meant to be working.

Distracted by technology, life often deprives us of moments of relaxation. But these little breaks are well worth reclaiming. Forget about working though lunch or sitting at your desk to eat. Make lunch an important time out. More than a moment for eating, this time offers an opportunity to change gears and briefly rest. Maybe it's not enough on its own, but everyone benefits from at least varying their pace and postures. By creating an event and engaging in the moment, we can at least clear our thoughts. That way, we can experience something close to rest.

Play fits in too. Having fun, enjoying being active, or having a good laugh with friends all count, don't they? Doing any of these is good recreation and, happily, they don't need much structure.

Giving you a natural lift, playing is a natural pick-me-up. Maybe a rest would be best, but the fun of play is also okay and a lot easier to explain than falling asleep in the back room.

Building opportunities for restoration throughout your day is wise living because saving it all for the weekend isn't enough. To balance the demands of daily life, you need resilience. Having habits that support your wellbeing increases your opportunity to feel good right now. Being a cornerstone to happiness, I encourage you to respect yourself and make room for rest. Doing so will build your health and hardiness; helping you cope whenever you feel dejected.

Surviving Depression

To me, anything you can do to increase your state of wellbeing is worth looking at. Perhaps because I've seen enough of despair to learn to value self-care.

Why raise depression in relation to everyday beauty? Well, in a good-looking world it doesn't seem to make sense, does it? But, as I keep reminding you, true beauty is at home in life just as it is. More importantly, beauty brings comfort where we can find no other.

Depression is a significant topic because its symptoms mirror existence without beauty. If you've gone through it then you know what I mean. Reducing our capacity to appreciate and create it brings a most intense dis-ease. Missing true beauty, no wonder depression is a journey into ugliness.

Struggling through discouragement at any time is hard of course. We know in our own way that life can be incredibly tough.

But when gloom begins dominating our days for prolonged periods, we enter a different realm. A place where beauty begins drifting away and where being and despairing have the same meaning. Simple things become outrageous challenges. Getting up in the morning and putting one foot in front of another to keep moving is a gargantuan struggle. Feeling hopeless, the world's colors silently drain away. Music plays but it brings no pleasure.

Unlike feeling down, depressive illness feels completely beyond our ability to switch it off. Controlling it is like trying to control a broken leg. Thankfully, most people are beginning to accept that. The last thing you need if you are experiencing depression is to feel ashamed for being sick.

Differing from breaks and bruises, brain-based illness have unwelcome side effects, don't they? A torn ligament will be painful but it won't dramatically affect your identity the way depression can. So it's not surprising others feel tentative about its effects. Add the fact depression can be concealed to the vague nature of moods and confusion is compounded. Unlike a wound you need to be open to it's telltale signs to notice it.

Cruelly, depressive illness resists its remedy. Having no hope, looking for beauty in anything seems utterly pointless. Creating anything worthy feels completely beyond you when depression descends. That is its sickness. Its symptoms keep stealing your satisfaction, so that the promise of happiness looks like an empty husk.

Gratefully, depression need not be final. By far, the majority of people recover. For those surviving its ill effects, I believe care plays a remarkably crucial factor.

Helpless as depressive feelings render you, I believe there is room for self-discipline. We can still go through the motions of keeping our days structured. Then at least we can simulate being okay. Sometimes, when there's a break in the clouds of gloom, we can even feel sunlight again.

Depression feels constant which, of course, is one of its symptoms. In reality, feeling low often fluctuates as moods rise and fall across each day.

Rather than completely shutting out the world, keeping close to the stream of daily life helps. Moments of appreciation or relief can happen just by being with people, pets, and nature. Spending time with others who know your needs and accept you can be a great comfort. As you instinctively know, togetherness helps.

Strategies allowing time out from responsibility are also beneficial. When you are not coping, an hour out of the action can be a blessing.

Compassionate medical and psychological treatment is a priority in every event. But, sometimes, even those giving support need backing up too.

If you know someone caught in the mud of depressive illness, your care can be a beautiful contribution. Caring transfuses beauty to someone who feels bereft. Staying close and accepting their need for support, therefore, is an intensely compassionate act.

Through appreciating and creating, you can tenderly bathe someone's life with your awareness. By expressing *The Seven Strengths*, you are creating a climate of hope. So never underestimate the healing ability you have. Even if you feel unsure of what you can give. Remember that wellbeing in itself has a health-giving influence.

Confronting Depression from Both Sides

My experience of depression has certainly been challenging. Many of the people we worked with through our rehabilitation consultancy suffered depression. Typically, it was the primary reason they were unable to work. Or they experienced it as a secondary symptom.

Years of experience with the effects of depressive illness gave me valuable insights but little preparation in helping me deal with myself.

Gradually, seemingly from nowhere, it appeared. Becoming increasingly shut down, Ruth noticed something was seriously wrong. As my low mood began intensifying, I started struggling to cope with even the most basic tasks. Getting dressed, preparing a sandwich, or answering the phone became hurdles.

Hour by hour, sometimes minute to minute, I fought emotions of overwhelming despair. My mood state kept insisting I would be better off dead. Crazy as it seems, it felt sensible, even rational. Everything I did felt utterly pointless.

Still, I kept going, resisting with nothing but willpower, as life got too difficult for me to explain.

Having reasons to live helped me fight my illness. The dry irony of helping clients deal with their depression was a joke too tragic to laugh about. Often I was in a worse state than they were. But going through the motions gave me focus. I kept working.

By their presence, Ruth, our two sons, and the staff kept reminding me that my depressive beliefs were somehow wrong. They needed me to live, so I had to keep living.

Possessing things that people feel are important would certainly not have been enough to keep me alive.

Dealing with so many doctors professionally, it was a little awkward finding one for myself. I didn't want to be a patient for someone I might also be working with as a consultant. But eventually I got past caring and saw a doctor at random.

Bad choice.

Diagnosing me as severely depressed, he sent me off with a drug prescription and promotional video, saying a high dose would sort me out.

It didn't. Things got worse.

Now, along with suicidal feelings, I began slipping into a dazed fog of complete confusion. I was both depressed and spaced out. Whenever someone spoke to me, I heard them as if from a distance. Constantly feeling like I was out of my body, everything became dulled. Sleeping and waking merged together into one dreary, dreamy state. Trying desperately to keep control, my head felt jammed full of cotton wool. Zoned out, I feared I was going mad. But there was nothing I could do. Nor could I properly describe it.

When I tried to explain, the doctor kept dismissing my symptoms, giving me well-intentioned pep talks instead.

To keep alive and sane, I kept reminding myself that my family needed me regardless. Even if I was sentenced to depression for the rest of my life, perhaps it would be slightly less damaging than taking my own life.

Talking about how I felt was too much. So I began using code to let Ruth know how I was coping. A "red card" day was very bad, meaning *"Don't leave me alone too long. I can barely bear being in my skin. The minutes are looming, and I'm counting down each one."*

A yellow card, on the other hand, was pretty good. *"Don't expect too much. But I'm here."* Orange covered everything in between.

In retrospect, it's amazing how reasonable you can still look while being out of your mind on medication. Despite having one hand hovering over my own doomsday button, most people never knew anything was wrong.

Two things got me through. Firstly, Ruth's beautiful encouragement kept reminding me why surviving was necessary. She kept telling me, over and over, that she wanted me to live. With nothing else to live for, I clung to her compassion.

Secondly, by drawing on my perseverance, I willed myself to survive. Though bereft of hope, sheer willpower kept insisting living was necessary. I'm glad determination overcame my distorted belief.

For a whole year, I existed like this, dangerously drifting between the red and yellow spectrums. Then we started looking for a second medical opinion. Realizing the situation, the second doctor immediately switched me over to another drug. The effect was dramatic. Two days later I came out of my drugged confusion. For the first time in twelve months, I could finally think clearly.

Best of all, I began recovering from my depression. Red card days became rarer. By the second year's end, I went off the medication completely. I became myself once more.

> *"You desire to know the art of living, my friend? It is contained in one phrase: make use of suffering."*
>
> Henri-Frederic Amiel

Having recovered totally I have often wondered what triggered it all. Like so many close calls in life, the experience has made me think a lot about happiness and the power of beauty in life (No doubt it's one of the reasons I'm writing to you now).

Being more philosophical I found it telling when, eighteen months later, the drug I was first prescribed was suddenly withdrawn from sale. Being implicated for causing a number of suicides, violent attacks, and other serious side effects, the medicine meant to "sort me out" briefly became an outrageous news headline before quietly being forgotten.

Facing desperation, life became precarious. But the beautiful qualities of *heart* and *fortitude* kept pulling me through. Ruth's encouragement, perseverance, and courage gave me sufficient support to carry on.

We all have moments of hardship, don't we? When you find yourself struggling in the pits of despair hold on tight to your beliefs. Use The Seven Strengths. Liberate the best that's in you and stand firm. Then, when everything else is stripped away, the character it reveals in you will show you what life is for.

Revealing You

You will understand, then, why I believe in being genuine and why indifference is so damaging. In trying to enthuse, some people stress the importance of a smile at all costs. *"Better an insincere smile than a sincere frown any day"* they say. To me that translates into *"better to live a phony life that looks good than a genuinely unhappy one."* This just appears to be another way of saying that revealing your true personality isn't adequate (unless it looks like plastic cheese).

Personally, I believe that sort of sentiment reflects ugly thinking. If we cannot face the reasons for our unhappiness, then we're never going to come out of it. Instead, we'll be condemned to hide our true nature under a mask of mock delight. That's not a way to live. That's a way to pretend. And that's a prison.

Being our best self is not about constantly acting hyper-gleeful or sickeningly nice. It's about being true to our selves and offering to others the best we can be at the time. If you were downhearted, then surely that would be an honest description of your feelings. Perhaps it's an awkward reality. But it would remain a dominating fact.

At least with the support of a friend or two, honest vulnerability could build positive intimacy and trust. Given we all have bleak times in our lives, there's something important about recognizing things as they are. It may not be popular, but it builds an *honesty* worth trusting.

Despite the message of our *make-me-happy-now* culture, dealing with things we would otherwise run from is generally beneficial. Why? Because difficulty drags us, sometimes kicking and screaming, to decisions we need to make.

Take the person who is always dismissing any sad feelings you have. They have an agenda, which says they can't face your pain. Yours raises the specter of theirs, which they're busy avoiding. Your emotional *honesty* is, therefore, just too threatening to handle.

How refreshing, then, to be in the company of someone who accepts you for you. Your feelings, whether up or down, don't faze her. Knowing herself, she is comfortable about you having feelings she doesn't choose.

Being in the presence of people like that reminds you that you have an identity worth revealing. Otherwise, being stifled by expectations and unspoken limits, we toe the line. *Don't say anything too frank because the truth is too touchy. Pretend to be interested because it smoothes things over.*

But dishonesty and appeasement without respect have undermining effects. What's so wrong about having our own opinions and feelings anyway? Why must be suppress ourselves?

I say, live boldly with love. Be true to what moves you, expressing your values through *The Seven Strengths*. Then exercise your acceptance, allowing for others to totally disagree if they want.

> **"Nothing can bring you peace but yourself."**
> Ralph Waldo Emerson

Coming out with the truth of your own thoughts, I believe, is both healthy and essential. We must be authentic to what is meaningful to us. Otherwise, we are living dead to ourselves. At the very least, you deserve your own loyalty. By daring to speak what you believe and live according to what you respect, you earn your own self-respect.

Grappling with low confidence earlier in my life, I have also witnessed it in countless others. We need to throw off apologizing for being ourselves. Claiming the freedom to be right and sometimes quite wrong is a privilege each of us share because we're human.

Some, of course, find this to be no hardship. For them it's unthinkable and absurd to hesitate being yourself. They not only get it, they live it. Like them, the rest of us need to start living it too.

Living beautifully right now can occur by happenstance, but usually it takes some thinking. When things start going awry, it obviously takes much more than a bright, smiley attitude to put everything right.

Going through trials by fire are no reason for us to hide. Rather, they show how much we need to develop. Focusing on our character, qualities, and sense of purpose is the simple yet challenging answer. For living beautifully there are no shortcuts.

Chapter 8

Conquering Emotional Chaos

"And you? When will you begin that long journey into yourself?"

Rumi

Emotionally Fit

When they're most confusing, emotions seem to bamboozle half of the population and torment the rest.

Everything we do is wrapped inside bundles of them. This, of course, is news to many men. Lured by the safety of logic, they believe anything that makes us feel too intensely is generally not to be trusted. So talking up emotion sets alarm bells ringing.

I've come across lots of men who laugh off emotional sensitivity or sidestep it completely as their default strategy. Remember all the jibes about real men and quiche? Well guys also prefer to keep their feelings tightly leashed.

Perhaps men aren't as well adapted for emotional expression. In the heat of the moment, many a man helplessly stalls, tongue-tied as he tries to tell his partner his true feelings. It's as if the male brain overloads. Rising like a tsunami, the emotional surf is completely overwhelming. Barraged by waves of panic, tenderness gets washed away, confirming yet again that feelings cannot be trusted.

Drawing out the emotionally constricted needs patience to progress. They need new words to describe their feelings. Labels to tag subtlety as well as strength. Even in good relationships, truthfully talking about emotions can be downright intimidating.

Why is this? And what are men thinking by denying the importance of feelings?

You know I'm generalizing here, of course. For the record, some men will find this totally untrue for them. Recognizing the situation, they are nonetheless exceptional. At least for the time being.

> *"You cannot teach a man anything. You can only help him discover it in himself."*
>
> Galileo Galilei

For lots of reasons, too many males are emotionally incapable. They live in what they feel is a rational way, treating everyone the way they treat themselves. Inside, their emotional realm is a tiny town inhabited by emotional stereotypes. Just as they have limited imagination for color ("What the heck is the difference between *Lavender* and *Orchid* anyway?"), their words for feelings are roughly restricted to *happy, sad, mad*, and *glad*. They dismiss ideas of beauty's importance as *weak* and *ridiculous*. In their eyes anything especially related to tender emotions should be distrusted. Making beauty a priority is way too feminine for them to accept.

Emotions are dangerous.

And it's true. Completely denying the value and quality of the emotional realm certainly makes beauty a threatening idea. It's safer to just bolt it down and dismiss it with a sexist label to put it in its place.

Right now, some of our leaders are preaching cold indifference. Yet, bizarrely, we accept their leadership.

We refuse to accept bungling in our leaders' logic. Their mistakes in *reasoning* become the subject of instant criticism. So why do we routinely put up with people in authority showing emotional incompetence?

Once installed they are hard to root out, remaining a frequent source of painful and costly conflict.

For now, emotional deficiency is endured and even ignored. For as long as it's tolerated, job descriptions will fail to flag it. Double talk will keep dismissing it, and the lack of compassion will persist, if not increase.

I wonder if this anguish over emotions comes from a fear of facing pain. Looking stoic may convey strength, but it might also have its origins in confusion, misdirection, and bluff. When it comes to being in charge, it's much easier to deny than cry.

So, unless our awareness changes, problems will remain. In business emotional denial will keep converting into high staff turnover and social damage. Emotionally illiterate community leaders will continue undermining their own best efforts. There won't be any planning behind this damage. Or even a lack of good intentions. Just pure, unadulterated inability. Leadership combined with emotional deficiency will simply keep translating into trouble. Until we decide to cap it together as a community, a legacy of abuse will keep pouring out. That's something no amount of politically correct promises can ever cure.

We need greater emotional awareness to reduce the damage. That's why there's never been a more pressing time to recognize the role of our emotional capacity. Together, we have the feeling ability to help each other and ourselves.

Hurting & Broken Hopes

Is there also a solution for lost hope? Right now, all around you, people are feeling overwhelmed with pain and suffering. Families and couples you know are struggling through deep anxiety with feelings they fear to face. Because someone won't talk disappointments are being suppressed. That's because talking it over is too threatening. So resentments are getting buried down deep. Not to heal, but to fester.

With so much pent-up emotional expression being restrained, resentments can abruptly bubble over into uncontrollable rage. For some, blocked goals will convert into frustration. Violence will

> *"Anger is never without reason, but seldom with a good one."*
>
> Benjamin Franklin

appear as if from nowhere. For someone you know, peace will disintegrate into shouting brutality. Then there will be others dear to you who, despairing, will simply take the shortcut into quiet, enveloping misery.

Right now, regardless of how you are feeling, you are completely surrounded by hurting people. Shouldering relationship pain, they keep it close to their chest. With pain that is too deep and too raw to reveal.

Though we experience it personally and recognize it immediately, suffering is more common than any of us would care to admit. Hiding behind facades of happy self-control, it stays secret, disguised behind masks of politeness, formality, and insistent independence.

Near where you live, there are children longing for honest love from their parents. Wives will be lying awake tonight, stricken with worry and sadness. Through the wee small hours, they'll be wondering how they got caught in such relationship loneliness. Silently yearning for rescue, they will dream of escaping. But there's nowhere to go.

I know when you're dying inside it's hard to put your mind to anything, much less acts of beauty. Living well gets a low priority when unresolved hurts take center stage. Joy gets pushed aside by self-pity. In *feel-sorry* moments we'll say, *"Having a beautiful life is for lucky people. Fine for them, but not for me."* Why? Because hurt is a dominating force. Until a chink of possibility finds its way through, thoughts of beauty get junked.

Finding solutions to emotional lockdown rests in relationship. Someone has to live *The Seven Strengths* for us to feel their power. By daring to open up and show our own vulnerabilities. Through choosing to take the time to shut up and listen. Just taking people as they are and accepting the positive silence of discovery. By deciding to reach out for no reward other than the satisfaction of living graciously. These are our answers to hurting and brokenness.

People in pain can look deceptively capable. But the fact is that none of us can find solace when we feel alone. We need real practical compassion. You need friends to love you beautifully through your

> *"I like living. I have sometimes been wildly, despairingly, acutely miserable, racked with sorrow, but through it all I still know quite certainly that just to be alive is a grand thing."*
> Agatha Christie

hurts, just as they need you. The more you do, the more fulfilling your connection.

Suffering is like a question waiting for an answer. Though often prickly and intimidating, there's no need to flee from distress. Be willing to give comfort and connection even if it's refused. Just being prepared to face and accept the pain of others is an act of beauty. When people are ready to believe in the acceptance of others, healing begins.

Forgive me if I'm making this sound neat and convenient because it isn't. Most often, it's awkward, and by trying to help, your kindness risks being misunderstood. So firmly anchor yourself by recognizing your own intrinsic value as a person. Let your *fortitude* and *giving* come from your own certainties. Stay within your confidence as far as you are able and keep standing strong on that.

Mood Swinging

When nobody else is responding, reaching out takes pluck. Beneath it needs to be a bedrock of belief that things can be better through our choices. Though naturally optimistic I do have my moments. My mood state fluctuates with the unfolding of each day. How much sleep I got last night, what I just ate, and whom I'm with are a big influence on my state of mind.

Realizing my emotions are up, down, and all over the place at times is intensely humbling. But instead of forcing myself to think positively, I work on being more aware of my mood from moment to moment. Just knowing my feelings color my decisions helps me think things through more evenly. Leastways, Ruth thinks I am one of the steadiest people she knows.

Whatever your mood, I believe it's wise to allow for other emotional possibilities than those you *feel* are true. Despite their supposed certainty, supreme pessimists and born optimists alike don't have the whole story. Allowing the possibility for things we don't know keeps us mindful that we need each other to see ourselves and our relationships better.

Being together helps keep our awareness evolving. With the benefit of differing opinions, we can get past our own internal weaknesses. Even things like bigger ideas can help put our shifting moods back in their box.

Maybe, in some perfect world, your emotional life, thoughts, and energies would remain stable. Yet isn't it strange that this is exactly what many of us expect from others?

It's normal for all of us to have ups and downs to some degree. Sometimes slight, sometimes enormous; the only thing we can be sure of is that we need to factor these shifts in.

Deciding in advance how to handle your "dangerous if mishandled" moods is a sensible strategy. Like storing unstable compounds, they need precaution rather than panic the moment they start spilling out. Take command with preparation then consciously aim for behavior you can accept, whatever the circumstances.

Because I become short-fused when I'm tired, I have one rule I strive to obey: shut up and enjoy the scenery. For me, distrusting my critical voice has come from a multitude of embarrassing experiences.

> *"Do not be too timid and squeamish about your reactions. All life is an experiment. The more experiments you make the better."*
>
> Ralph Waldo Emerson

So find what works for you. Making the most of your mood is part of smart living. Using self-understanding you have the ability to figure out the *wisdom* of your ways at every level. Like mining your past experiences, think of it as harnessing another valuable reserve.

The power of this kind of self-awareness is immediately obvious. When you feel most vulnerable, plugging into your emotional patterns helps you cope. You can boost your self-approval simply by recognizing the predictability of your behavior.

Admitting you need to withdraw when overwhelmed rather than

pushing through and falling into a heap later is liberating. Creating new habits also lets you cope with your lower moments. Just as having a grab bag of ways to short circuit your irritability makes you a more pleasurable person to be with.

Being awake to your moods and inner motivations also gives you greater composure. Otherwise, the alternative is to remain at their mercy, being repeatedly tossed about like a rowboat in an endless sea of mood states.

> *"Denial ain't just a river in Egypt."*
> Author unknown

Some would say, "Well, that's natural." But, at its extreme, I would say it's unhelpful. Regularly expressing our emotions without some form of self-checking is a pattern of powerlessness. Natural as they are, our sentiments can be both a blessing and a bane. So anything that drives us to mechanically react deserves reflection.

Feeling unable to change things generally stems from an inner blindness. As difficulties beset us, our inability to see within ourselves only compounds frustration. Applying more self-discipline, working even harder, or shrinking into denial purely makes things worse. Trying to pretend or dismiss our bad moods away is also futile. Come the next big emotional meltdown, the effort generates self-sabotage.

Without growing self-awareness, living more beautifully with our emotions will always be a rollercoaster. Freedom relies on us seeing our ways with *honesty* and a generous sweep of reason. Examining what's behind our emotions not only allows us occasional insights, it's destined to be an eye-opening experience of personal breakthroughs. So long as we realize the fickle nature of our thinking.

Rational Only Sometimes

It is amazing how much of what drives us is actually so prone to impulse and whim. Though we like to paint ourselves as levelheaded, our senses, drives, and emotions typically take priority. For instance, how do you choose the best paint colors? And how will you pick your next outfit? If you're feeling hungry, what will you decide to eat, and why?

Despite being widely considered as essential, rational thinking fails to embrace much of the subtleness of our daily behavior. Even our biggest life decisions are shaped beyond logical thinking. Who chooses their life partner or friends based on logic?

Whilst we might try to make decisions through practical reasoning, we cannot simply dismiss or ignore our emotions without penalty. Take grocery shopping. Despite trying to be as practical as possible and working to a strict budget, marketing gurus always see us coming. Promoting certain products as offering the *best value* and being *the most sensible choice* is persuasive. Knowing emotions of confidence matter, they give products a reassuring glow.

So how much of our shopping baskets is influenced by the emotional appeal embedded in each brand? Maybe you're stronger than me, but when I go shopping, I know I'll be driven by wanting to please Ruth, our kids, the cats, and any potential guests. So I'll be driven by a desire to provide the best I can afford.

Those in the retail game know that regardless of a product's features, emotion inevitably outsells everything else. Politicians know too, promising security after first milking our fears. We want the facts, but we are swayed by our feelings. Passionate emotion can inspire us to commit our lives to each other. And even lay them down.

> **"As soon as you trust yourself, you will know how to live."**
> Johann Wolfgang von Goethe

But if passion is not backed by deeper substance all the emotional zeal in the world won't stop it from falling apart. When things start changing, emotions destabilize. The mood gripping us so convincingly yesterday can just as easily fall away today. When that prized new dress starts coming loose at the seams or your treasured pet starts shredding your couch, emotions go from standby calm to arm waving, tongue-flapping hysteria.

There has to be something more than the strength of our feelings to endure the test of time. If we don't want to be slaves to constant reaction, then we need to have reasons to hold firm. To protect ourselves from the restlessness of emotional swings takes *decision*.

Perhaps the best conclusion we can make is that all we feel is not all there is. There are layers to our behaviors. Just as the source of our distress is not always what it seems.

Casting Shadows

Psychological defense mechanisms are another layer of our sophistication and how we handle our feelings reveals their complexity. There's often a tangle of them caught between our true views and what we actually express. Then when realities and emotions clash we apply them, performing mental gymnastics, to justify why. As demanding as it is, this feat happens almost automatically.

For the sake of being right, everything that doesn't fit about our thoughts goes into hiding. Yet the more we try looking good, the more the opposite secretly appears. For those hankering for life balance, it all starts with coming to terms with your contradictions.

Where denial keeps reigning, there's a part of us that's out of control. Emotions get the upper hand in ways we don't expect. Even concealing our feelings to make ourselves seem serene won't hold them back forever. When emotions do come out, the intensity they carry can be surprising. Cascading in torrents of tears or outbursts or rage, they bubble up to the surface with overwhelming force.

Sometimes appearing in disguise, these emotional drivers manifest an abundance of behaviors. They can even direct our whole way of life.

As long as our driving forces stay in our blind spots, they have the potential to continue wreaking havoc. Distanced from them, we can live as if they have nothing to do with us. Being unable to see them, we can hide from the harm they inflict.

Perhaps it's our fear of disapproval that causes our blindness. Telltale signs can be seen in our projections. But anything too hot to touch upon, particularly anything seen as a moral issue, gets projected elsewhere. Instead of awkwardly facing our failings firsthand, inferiorities and hatreds start finding scapegoats.

As our closeted self casts scrutiny toward others, blame is safely diffused and dished out elsewhere.

> *"Everything that irritates us about others can lead us to an understanding of ourselves."*
>
> Carl Jung

To the extent we project, we criticize in others what is really the image of our own shadow. Keeping ugliness at arm's length, we can safely hate it without having to come in contact with it. By disowning it in our own behavior, we can righteously feel disgusted by the awful conduct of others.

The greater the pressure to be good, the more we judge others by their lack of it. Believing we need to be thoroughly nice every day might compel us to displace our embarrassment. It has to go somewhere, doesn't it? Directing focus toward someone else's nastiness is much easier to endure than recognizing nastiness in ourselves. Like all Hollywood heroes, we need our own set of baddies to keep showing how good we are.

Whilst the payoff of blaming is powerful, it can also be psychologically draining, sapping a lot of mental energy. The bigger the problem projected, the more effort expended. Translating into a whole range of symptoms, it can manifest as exhaustion, headaches, and a variety of afflictions. The lengths we will go to transfer it all are remarkable.

Telling an intimidated victim, for instance, that they have also been bullying is highly confronting. As if hit with a fist, they may appear shocked, affronted, and then angry. Quickly plugging their internal story back together, they may attempt to reassert their role as the sufferer.

Similarly, when a racist bigot is reminded of their foreign ancestry, they may be surprised and discomforted by the idea. Then, quickly trucking out a standard line that it's different, they retreat to their inside story.

Shaking up false beliefs by being confronting might work in therapy, but it doesn't seem very effective in normal conversation.

How sobering is it that our hostility to people different from us is tied to our projected failings? Complaining loudly about other people's greed and indifference means I can still avoid facing my

> *"Fear of something is at the root of hate for others, and hate within will eventually destroy the hater."*
>
> George Washington Carver

own. Transferring it beyond me also makes me feel a lot safer. I don't have to face myself if I take it out on someone else. Even if someone sees through my disguise, my head-in-the-sand approach means they must have a problem too. Better to turn up the blowtorch another notch on the bad guys instead.

If I ever put it all together, I could finally shut the projection down. But first that means changing the script of my internal tale. Firstly, I need to know I am just as bad and good as anyone else who has ever walked before me. Then, knowing I don't need to hold anyone's fort, push their barrow, or stand guard for the side, I can let go. If I really comprehend this, I can accept it and be humble.

So what are the signs we're casting shadows? Well, obsessing over the failings of others is common. Expressing undue anger that *"they're at it again"* is a clue. Feeling an overriding hostility about people because they are different. Or repeatedly moralizing, blaming, or experiencing simmering aggression raises a red flag.

As a rule of thumb, reacting excessively points to projecting behavior. But it's hard to be too specific about what we are unknowingly trying to hide.

What's more, this is all incredibly discomforting to voice. Realizing that some of the problems of life are stemming from ourselves is shaming. Becoming aware can leave us embarrassed, confused, and feeling more than a bit bruised. It hurts. Facing our failings and the reality of our resentments is a stinging encounter. But it also brings freedom. Freeing ourselves from the burden of judging also means we need to give ourselves a double scoop of self-acceptance to compensate. It's hardly a pleasant step, but growing through this is a beautiful experience.

Now you may be wondering what this has got to do with you. But I encourage you to give this plenty of consideration all the same. Maybe you don't have any projecting behaviors. But considering this possibility is a healthy way of fine-tuning your awareness.

To satisfy yourself think about talking this over with someone you respect. If you feel there are major issues needing to be addressed, consider professional counseling to resolve them.

With humble honesty and awareness, we can all break through our limiting patterns. Knowing our selves enough to choose our truest nature is so thoroughly satisfying that it is worth the time and effort to achieve. The alternative is to be driven by forces of fear we cannot control, leaving us disconnected and discomforted.

Feeling Fear

In every instance, living in fear is a diminishing experience. Undermining our desire for reaching out and exploring creativity, it imprisons us in perpetual uncertainty.

Wrapped in a variety of guises, some fears are easy to spot. Others are completely unexpected. But, recognized or not, they all come with dire consequences.

For those with heightened fears of rejection, engaging socially becomes a seemingly insurmountable hurdle. Given a choice they'd rather pass up a social invitation than pass out from the anxiety of meeting somebody new.

Meanwhile those fearing change believe any shift means daunting uncertainty to be avoided at all costs. Like clothing that's gotten so tight it restricts nearly all movement, old ways may be difficult to shed. But at least their familiarity is consoling.

Fears also have something else in common. They always foresee loss. Fearing intimacy, rejection, or failure, we believe our sense of self will be irreparably eroded.

When I was a child, my parents would sometimes take us to the local doctor's clinic in a run-down art deco house on a busy road. Going at nighttime we'd sit inside the cheerless waiting room. At least that's what they called the old converted porch. Sitting there I looked up in dread at the round-windowed door leading into the doctor's surgery. Hidden behind its frosted glass, came the sounds of murmuring and low moaning. What terrifying secrets lay within? I imagined the white-coated doctor, intent on inflicting pain. Why, oh why, did we have to see this terrible man? By injecting, slicing, prodding, and poking, I was sure he was a torturer in disguise.

Though not recalling all that much about the treatment, I vividly remember being scared to death. My lifelong fear of round windows, especially ones with frosted glass, keeps reminding me how forcefully fright captures imagination.

Regardless of the facts, negative expectations can be crippling, drastic, and difficult to defeat. That's why fear of failure not only blocks people doing their best. It stops them trying in the first place. The underlying belief that their goal is impossible to achieve saps their motivation completely.

Fearing success, on the other hand, gets its power by stealth. Carrying this invisible cudgel, people strike their own hand just as achievement nears. Mysteriously pulling the pin on their plans, they hesitate. Behind conscious awareness, feelings of unworthiness have a devious way of triggering self-sabotage.

> **"Worry gives a small thing a big shadow."**
>
> Swedish proverb

Deep down beneath fears like these is something strangely rewarding. Proving we don't deserve success or that people really despise us, we can at least show we are right. This idea, somehow, seems to be incredibly important to us. With our radar tuned toward confirming our beliefs, we tend to get what we expect. Even if it means shooting ourselves in the foot to prove it.

That's why getting to know the whys behind your fears is so worthwhile. Becoming aware of yourself in action as if you were a casual observer is particularly beneficial. Think about how things have come to be in your life. How do they trigger your reactions? Sometimes that's all it takes to help you move on. But if you need more insight, do whatever it takes to get more.

If getting professional help means living more beautifully, do it. You deserve it.

Instead of leaving them buried beneath surface confidence, start bringing your anxieties out. Living in an emotional prison is a waste of a good life. So make breaking free a top priority and start taking over.

Begin to look closely and you'll see personal doubts are frequently not much more than the loose ends of dismal questions. Few fears are founded on facts. Instead, they hang around, niggling and blocking our view. Each anxiety is holding you back from being your best.

Deliberately face a fear and you start tackling it. Meaning any fear that keeps you down, preventing you from being your whole self, can be conquered.

> *"You gain strength, courage, and confidence by every experience in which you really stop to look fear in the face.*
>
> *You must do the thing which you think you cannot do."*
>
> Eleanor Roosevelt

First comes facing. Then comes deciding, which already brings benefits. Choosing to push through apprehensions can boost your self-opinion to the stratosphere. That's because your inner you is closely watching what you do. Push through, and she will admire you for daring to do what you've feared most.

The saying *"Fear knocked on my door one day, and when I opened, it ran away"* tells us we need to confront these nasty nuisances head-on. Often, under the weight of our conscious scrutiny, groundless fears easily collapse. Leaving behind the original cause, we can pop them into a mental box and get rid of them for good. When you are ready to challenge your fears, a new level of life will suddenly become yours for the taking.

Of course, advising is much easier than doing. I have had to will myself to defeat fear because being brave isn't my natural default setting. I choose and keep choosing it under sufferance. Things like public speaking leave me dizzy, dry-mouthed, and desperately grasping for excuses. Repeated reasoning never brings a cure for me. But doing overcomes it.

Throwing so many fears overboard over the years, I have come to believe we can all do just about anything (though my lack of facial hair crushes my career in the World Beard and Moustache Championships).

When I was growing up, Mama's anxieties created a readymade climate of fear that I easily adopted. She readily feared the worst and always managed to convey it in vivid Technicolor. Even if I stood on a kitchen chair, she'd be pleading with me not to fall. So, naturally I developed a fear of heights.

Fearful of teachers I began stuttering in high school whenever I talked to them. Though I enjoyed learning, I quailed at the thought of failure in school. This wasn't so remarkable seeing as I dreaded disapproval of any kind. Feeling anxious for most of my life, I kept biting my nails and trying to hold in my fears. But I also did something right. I decided to press on regardless.

That's how I've learned about the freedom of choosing. I still fight my shyness. Group photos often find me hiding behind a tree (not quite, but almost). At least it gives my children a laugh. They wonder at Dad's contradictions. On the one hand, to right retail injustice he can calmly face open hostility. On the other, he'll avoid asking a sales assistant for help so as not to be a bother.

Opening the door to fear is an act of sheer will. First you must reason with yourself that your fear is essentially irrational. Then, fighting hesitation, you must not only open the door but also get out and chase your fears down the road. Daring myself to do what my fears screamed I could not, I:

- Began climbing high ladders for cherry picking then went on to climb some cliffs (Now I'm pretty good on a kitchen chair, and I live next to a cliff).
- Climbed a mountain alone on a stormy night without a light (Curing any fears I had of the dark).
- Worked as a salesperson to learn how to speak (I'm still speaking, and I'm still learning).
- Chose a job that involved changing adults' diapers (Any fears about getting my hands dirty shortly dissipated).
- Went to university, despite leaving school at sixteen (It taught me to give everything you've got your best shot).

- Learned to face a class of hostile teens (It's a bit like facing a firing squad without the comfort of a blindfold, but I found courage focusing on their needs, not mine).
- Left a job and went into business (Risk, in the right dose, is definitely a healthy thing).
- Developed new skills and qualifications to work with professionals and executives (Fear quickly surrenders to the demands of experience, hard work, and results).

Are these things momentous? No. But for me each choice was affirming. Each reminded me that fear is not an answer but an obstacle to overcome.

So I know first-hand that refusing to confront what frightens you only affirms your anxiety. Unchecked, the constant drip-drip of self-doubt drains you. Made serfs under the reign of fear, we go to great lengths avoiding and distracting ourselves. We will do anything to avoid facing what we dare not admit.

That's why, I believe, if fear is blocking you from doing something important, there is no other way. You must tackle it somehow. Your physical and mental health hinges on your willingness to face distress. Concealed in your anguish, I believe, are the keys to what you are missing.

Of course, becoming more of your good self takes *fortitude*. Even if it's not a lot, you've got to keep on developing what you've got. Giving more and having more means some things need changing. But how do we get past our fears when we feel blocked by their grid locking effects? One way is to build gradually and start talking it up. No need to be sudden or extreme (unless you want to be). Growing can be as fast, progressive, or subtle as you choose. Think about your temperament and hunt for clues on deciding your path. We all have a different coping level for adapting. So work with it rather than against it.

Just remember that daring to be your wonderful self is what living a beautiful life is about. Whatever the obstacles, do this one thing and it will begin to change everything.

I dare you.

Knowing Loneliness

Like fear, loneliness also has a deconstructing effect. Being friendless and lonely is something everybody has known at some point. It's a modern day scourge we seem to have accepted.

> *"One may have a blazing hearth in one's soul, and yet no one ever comes to sit by it."*
>
> Vincent Van Gogh

Cut off from meaning and adrift without friendship, everything we do falls to the level of joyless survival. Just eating, sleeping, and doing more work, we labor to live. Under the weight of loneliness, life becomes a mechanical meting out of tasks. We count the minutes, longing for an escape to yet more emptiness.

This slow-moving pain shows the depth of our need for each other. Relationship offers sustenance for the soul, and just like our need for food, we crave relationship in all the familiar flavors. That's a good thing. So I say to you: find your favorite ways and enjoy them all. Often.

If that's not possible, find simple gratitude within. Consider people you admire and contemplate those possessions you appreciate. You know only too well the negatives of your life. Now switch focus. What positives would a dedicated optimist be discovering if they were in your skin?

The obstacle is self-focus. As long as we remain trapped in self-absorbed thinking, we live self-imprisoned lives of solitary confinement. Perhaps not taking ourselves too seriously is a good road out. For some, simply forgetting to think and getting on being busy is enough to keep them going. Picking the best route depends a lot on how we tick.

But the passion of our sad urgings can only find true peace through the cure of company. As loneliness stokes its own cold flame, things only worsen. Unless we initiate change.

Waiting for rescue is wishful but wasted living. So if pangs of loneliness keep stalking, reach out. Find people with greater needs and offer healing by helping. With so much untapped emotional energy to release, *giving* can be a profound rush.

Discover new ways of engaging, especially with those needing help. Start today, as good things deserve to be actioned now. Allow yourself the opportunity to move on from the grief of a starving heart through the beauty of *giving*.

> **"The worst loneliness is not to be comfortable with yourself."**
>
> Mark Twain

By consciously transforming your pain into compassion, your feelings take on a positive direction. Letting your loneliness drive you to help someone needier than yourself connects you with beauty. Then, knowing and understanding the full pain of your own hurt, you can act with *heart*. Doing this you'll find all the nourishing you need. In *giving*, we get.

There's also something else. Amidst lack and longing, hope surfaces through the spring of gratitude. Expressing thankfulness is a beautiful thing made more precious by the difficulty of your circumstances. Heal yourself, as much as you can, by keeping gratefulness close to your heart. Then offer it to any who will gladly receive it.

If you are hurting, meet your own pain with kindness to yourself. Being isolated does not mean you have to disregard your own needs too. Show tenderness to yourself even when no one else will.

Yearning has its own restless energy, which you may as well channel and refine. Let it propel you to tackle tasks requiring sorting and rearranging. Perhaps you have a garden needing tender loving care. Or your cupboards need the clearing you've been promising for years.

> **"They are never alone that are accompanied with noble thoughts."**
>
> Sir Philip Sidney

Often big jobs get left to last because we feel they take too much effort. But with strong emotion as the engine, you can master more than you can imagine. Harness your feelings for results you can feel good about.

Naturally this means fighting upstream. It takes willpower to get things moving. Pushing feelings into something practical can feel foreign at first. Wanting to feel better, you might even feel worse. Feeling unmotivated means you must face the prospect of your own resistance. But if you ever want to lower its intensity, you must engage. Get into some heavy physical activity like rearranging the furniture or giving your surroundings a shine to prove you can do things. I call it domestic therapy.

Pulling Through Grief

Though loneliness and grief are often lumped together, their difficulties present very different experiences.

When Papa passed away, it was fascinating seeing how some people reacted to my loss. When I told one friend my father had just died, she barely skipped a beat. Instead of offering condolences, she continued talking enthusiastically about her shopping experiences. Though I knew she heard, she decided to act as if nothing had happened. It was as if her ability to relate at a deep emotional level had completely ceased to exist.

> *"If you're going through hell, keep going."*
> Winston Churchill

Similarly, others would pause, saying something like *"Sorry to hear that"* or *"That's a shame,"* and then simply continue their conversations. It reminded me of a powerful law. Whenever people are experiencing strong emotions, we need to acknowledge their existence. Whether they are bereaved, troubled, or deliriously happy, showing we accept someone's feelings validates them. Acceptance is a persuasive tool in bridging our relationship gaps.

From an earthly perspective, losing my father made me increasingly conscious of the finality of life. It kept troubling me. Flashbacks of his lifeless face plagued my sleep.

Death's locked door worried me. I don't know why, but even years later, it kept weighing on my mind.

Finally, one afternoon, I realized something vital. Dying and its trauma are just part of the frame of a lifetime. Like a mounted portrait, birth and death form the highlighting framework. They are meant to make us reflect on a whole life lived.

Dramatic as the frame might look, its importance comes from the person and their character. Death is nothing more than the edge of a life we've known. Magnifying our memories, it wraps them with final meaning; the whole portrait is compelling.

Transforming someone's flesh and blood life into something to reflect upon rather than react to is given to us in grief. We learn to preserve the person as a continuing identity who exists regardless of their physical absence. The more we see of them, the more grieving loosens its grip.

No sooner did I grab these things that I felt immediate release. Finally my grief eased. My brooding thoughts of death disappeared, and I let my father go.

Grief, I concluded, is a harsh teacher that we are obliged to respect. Surviving pain and loss demands we gain new awareness and face pain head-on. Forget about keeping things in to be brave. There is nothing indulgent or weak about grief.

More than that, this pit of loss can even have a health-giving function. Sorrow can encourage restructuring and restoration as old ways stop working. Grieving is therefore a natural forerunner for new beginnings. Challenging familiar habits, pain-sharpened senses cast a different light on everything.

Being tested by grief's torment is nobody's choice. Yet this is where we all must go to develop. We fear it. Even dread it. But ultimately you and I both must pass through it.

When Frank, a former client of mine, lost his wife to cancer, he immediately plunged into deep grief.

Within a week, however, he was back to work, trying to move on with life. Although wanting to get on with the job, he still felt immensely distressed.

Three months after the funeral, Frank's workmates started figuring it was about time Frank got over his grief. They started telling him to get a grip, be brave, and put it all behind him. Some suggested he start thinking about meeting somebody new.

Frank tried taking their advice. Though it meant suppressing his true feelings, he felt that he was at least doing *something*.

In the following months, no one spoke to Frank about his wife's death. But life was beginning to get back to normal anyway. Then something unexpected started happening. Frank began acting differently. Becoming increasingly forceful, the quiet, agreeable Frank was getting aggressive. And annoying. In fact, Frank was beginning to get under everyone's skin.

What Frank and his workmates were missing was that grief couldn't be dismissed when it is inconvenient. Repressing his strong feelings merely squeezed them out somewhere else. In this case, Frank slipped into shouting and threatening behavior.

Fortunately Frank's sister understood him well. With *wisdom* she translated his behavior and got him talking about the grief he was burying. Before the year was out, he commenced counseling. Reducing his pent up anger, Frank was able to share his feelings safely and openly. Though his loss was unavoidable, he found a way of moving on with living.

Despite the best of intentions, trying to put things away that haven't been dealt with only makes matters worse. No mental box is adequate for containing unresolved grief.

Facing personal loss can certainly be devastating. But experiencing someone else's grief can raise a whole lot of complex feelings. Aside from the obvious difficulties, sensitivities can make things delicate. Struggling to deal with our own discomfort can leave us uncertain about helping others and ourselves. That in itself becomes a hurdle. For this task we need the guiding of *heart, honesty, fortitude*, and *wisdom*. More often than not, when people are overwhelmed and grieving, compassion and sincerity are gratefully received.

Compare that with saying nothing. Avoiding or ignoring someone's loss can be unwittingly cruel. By refusing to honestly connect, feelings of isolation are reinforced. The silence of denial and avoidance can so easily be mistaken for shunning indifference.

> *"If you haven't any charity in your heart, you have the worst kind of heart trouble."*
>
> Bob Hope

Coming to terms with painful realities means being honest about any false sympathies we could offer. We need to be sensitive but genuine too. After all it's not as if someone grieving doesn't know what has happened. If anything, they expect us to be aware. Being upfront with our care and quiet, accepting presence can make a profound difference.

Listening, accepting, and calmly getting on with being helpful does have significance. So forget about asking if there is something you can do. Just think things through and respectfully help. You cannot fix their hurting, but you can be there for them. By letting ourselves relax, we can help grieving take its course.

Sorrow is a rocky, wearisome road. Intense grief can be so emotionally taxing that helpers need to find support too. So if you are in this role, be willing to seek help and take time out when you need it. That way, the care and rest you receive will keep sustaining you too.

By keeping a level head amidst all the emotion of grieving, you give something valuable that people need to grasp; a feeling of much needed security.

Crossing through grief, some people think it's their duty to be doling out judgment and hard-bitten advice. Perhaps reacting to their own insecurities, they refuse to give grief permission to exist and be felt. Fearing tenderness will merely fan the flames, they mistakenly insist that everyone should toughen up. But caring never deepens loss. It merely allows expression.

Sorrowing over a baby's death, whether through miscarriage or stillbirth, often meets uncomfortable silence. Sometimes the response is complete dismissal.

"Just get on with it and start again," *"It was never meant to be,"* or *"Just get over it"* are commonly said with the best of intentions. Even women who have known the same loss themselves will offer rehearsed condolences.

But if we value beauty, we will not despise raw feelings. It is a beautiful gift to let people grieve safely in our presence. Allowing people space to mourn will not prolong their loss. But pushing people away because we cannot deal with their pain remains profoundly wounding.

In a world marked with harshness and indifference, we have something to offer that is rare and precious. With *heart* we can bring the beauty of kindness to life. Together, with understanding, we can play an intimate role in making healing happen.

These issues are a part of life and the realm of emotion is where we belong. To take our feelings away or dismiss them strips an integral part of our humanity. Instead, they need recognition, and the power of the Seven Strengths to harness and discern their passion.

Chapter 9

Working Beautifully

"Never permit a dichotomy to rule your life, a dichotomy in which you hate what you do so you can have pleasure in your spare time. Look for a situation in which your work will give you as much happiness as your spare time."

Pablo Picasso

Matching Aptitude in the First Place

If you have the ideal job already and love how it fits in your life, congratulations! I have nothing more to add.

If you don't, read on.

Despite our best intentions, many of us keep finding ourselves in jobs that aren't us. Why do you think that's so? Is it because we don't feel we have the luxury of picking and choosing? Or are we just unsure of what we want?

Finding a workplace match draws far more from focus than good fortune. Like choosing clothes, it's all too easy to grab something because it's appealing. Then, we end up having to make allowances for the slightly awkward feeling later.

Day in, day out work that's ill-fitting gets downright uncomfortable. So it pays to plan ahead whenever you plan on making a job change.

Given we spend so much valuable time working, I believe this choice deserves careful consideration and systematic written scrutiny. Kind of like a resume but just for you to read.

> *"Choose a job you love, and you will never have to work a day in your life."*
>
> Confucius

Firstly, it's obvious we all have a natural leaning toward certain job fields. So excluding job opportunities because they wouldn't *feel right* is totally sensible. But more than that, I would also recommend considering your values. Write them down too. Then list your work experience. Thinking of tasks you have done capably in and out of your work, make a point list of your abilities. For instance you might handle complaints politely or follow through on tasks promptly without being reminded. If they influence your work, write them down.

You can then factor in your formal education too. Then, list the jobs your parents and siblings have held. This background can help give you a feel for the suitability of a potential role.

If you already have a range of work possibilities in mind, try jotting them down too. Compare them with your profile of values and background. Make a note of where things fit and where they don't.

The point of these steps is to help you in building a profile of your history that relates to your fields of interest. Your values, skills, and background provide the clues to finding a better match. At the very least, looking for patterns to help make sense of your future options will help you make better choices.

But looking at types of jobs is only one part of the story of course. Narrowing down your job preferences leads to the next step: finding the right employer for you.

Like any sovereign nation, every workplace also has its own culture. Each is like a world in itself. After being hired you could begin noticing unexpected attitudes and approaches. Some might delight you whilst others could come as a rude awakening.

I find it fascinating that there can be such major social contrasts between firms operating in the same street, let alone the same industry. One can be warm and inviting whilst another functions under knife-edged tension.

Frequently it begins with the boss's values. If you've been working in paid employment, you will have firsthand experience of this yourself.

Some workplace cultures will clearly fit you better than others. You could be in the right job for your skills but the wrong workplace for your values. Ordinarily you can pick this up at your first interview. But sometimes the culture clash is concealed under complex layers, hidden in unspoken expectations or the behavior of the staff. This is not to say that a particular culture is necessarily wrong. Just that we get the feeling we don't quite belong.

Sometimes the core task itself might only be a partial match. If so, you can harbor feelings of anxiety and self-doubt about your job. Besides never fully settling in, the experience can keep on undermining all the good you can do. That's why you need to have a good understanding of *You, Inc*. What kind of services and skills do you have to offer? What can you give that's way above average? And how much are you willing to learn? Knowing your capabilities and preferences improves your prospects of securing work that fits your strengths.

Next comes what you are willing to learn to do well. The limits of your ability are not set in your past but what you *want* to do.

Maybe carving out a brilliant career is your thing. Or perhaps you'd be happy just paying the bills. From the kick off point of your wants, you can build fulfillment by doing something worthwhile.

Finding Fulfillment

More than making us busy, work can get involved, can't it? Within each workday lies a world of motivations. Some see the whole thing as just a quest for more money. But you already know there's more to work than getting paid. Wherever possible we want to be doing things we believe in, performing tasks that suit our personality. We also value being part of something bigger than ourselves. So to be satisfying, work needs to involve us in a common cause. Be it worthwhile widget-making or helping provide a service, most people crave the feeling of being involved.

> *"To find out what one is fitted to do, and to secure an opportunity to do it, is the key to happiness."*
>
> John Dewey

The more fulfilling the process, the more it motivates. Financial needs aside, most of us expect more than money alone to get us out of bed. We want our efforts to count.

Sometimes being appreciated is the icing we desire. Even if we keep coping without it. But so long as our tasks and workplace relationships have meaning, work will keep us coming back for more.

Time wise, people normally think of work requiring a set amount of hours on the job. But what about factoring in preparation time? After all, you do all that psyching up for work and organizing to get out the door. Not to mention all of your commuting time. Later, there's even more time taken up by the activities you might do trying to switch off a working mindset. This means work takes up a huge portion of your life.

That's why, as I've said, it's an important step to think about finding work that best suits you. Choosing a job just because it is available is okay in the short term if unemployment is the only other option[1]. In the long term, you owe it to yourself to find work that reflects what matters to you. Again, if you've got that, fantastic! If not, I believe it's worth finding greater job satisfaction. In this way you can use your job to bring out your beautiful best and be happy now.

Compare that with the frustration of being stuck in a go nowhere position. Tragically, there are countless people trapped in jobs they detest. Caught by a rising tide of financial responsibilities and dwindling confidence, a popular fallback is to cave into a *hang in there* mentality. Hoping to keep everything afloat long enough, the aim becomes safely reaching the welcoming shores of retirement. Having enough health and funds to finally enjoy happier times is the secret dream sustaining many of us.

---

[1] *This is a big subject. So if you wish to discuss it in more depth, simply drop by www.happy.fm and share your thoughts.*

Justifiably, being caught in this bind makes us prone to disappointment and underperformance. Unhappy, we feel forced to work, injecting us with a daily dose of discouragement.

Such satisfaction-sapping work feeds a cynical view of beauty and the belief that real life is a grind.

Securing a job, therefore, where your best efforts count and you experience fulfillment is more than a bonus. It's liberation.

How do you find that kind of ideal work? Well let's add more to your profile. Think about what gets you going. Identify the kind of activities that inspire and capture your imagination because these are wonderful clues. If possible keep expanding your written list of career interests to broaden your possibilities. Consider short-listing any tasks you'd consider doing as a volunteer too.

Getting there might be hard or it might be easy. But real progress starts with recognizing your strengths. Knowing what you've got gives you more to go on than merely fishing around seeing what pops up in job advertisements.

> *"To find joy in work is to discover the fountain of youth."*
>
> Pearl S. Buck

You could also consider a career counselor to help guide you towards your ideal occupation. Try finding one in your neighborhood for starters. A good career counselor can reveal your talents. Despite what some people think, everyone has *some*. But if you prefer, I can also help. Feel free to get in touch through *www.happy.fm*. Because there is nothing like finding a more satisfying career to build your fulfillment.

Doing what you love brings untold contentment, and with passionate effort, good things keep coming. So if you are feeling hemmed in right now, knowing your situation just isn't working for you, I want to reassure you. Regardless of all of your responsibilities, you deserve to find fulfillment in your work. Dare to dream of possibilities instead of obstacles. Consider forming an action plan to improve things while minimizing risk. Maybe getting some study under your belt will boost your options. Perhaps start doing some voluntary work to test the waters. Change can be both scary and exciting. Review obstacles, but don't dwell on them. More than anything else, your motivation is the key to overcoming your deficits.

Worthwhile Working

Although they grab our attention, momentous events are, by nature, too rare to wait for. Yet by comparison our regular routines and tasks get far less recognition. Having a beautiful life right now can only happen if we look differently at what we are doing today. In this moment. In an hour. Or first thing tomorrow. *Revering* lets you find beauty in your life as it is. Just as *kindling* lets you create it, you know that if you choose it, beauty can appear in the familiar. From the humdrum of daily life, you understand that even the smallest moments can be made magnificent.

So why should something dominating the bulk of our time and attention be any different? Work holds a vast reserve of opportunities that often remain untapped.

Depending on our experience, work evokes a slew of emotions and opinions. Asking about someone's job triggers anything from glowing praise to audible moaning and head shaking. We understand these responses because, whatever our own view, we know work is challenging. Both its opportunities and its frustrations weave into our lives, uniting us all with its defining thread.

> *"Happiness comes when your work and words are of benefit to yourself and others."*
> Buddha

But seriously, bringing beauty into our work world? Merely mentioning beauty and work together is liable to get some confused stares. Work *and* beauty? Surely that's a mismatch. Doesn't beauty work best if kept to our home and social life?

If work is mechanically reduced to money, our efforts get retranslated too. The job market's unwritten rules imply you measure positive potential with wealth. At first that seems reasonable enough. Then the ugliness becomes glaringly obvious. Dignity, purpose, and qualities of beauty don't have an exchange rate. Whenever work misses the worth of the humanity in our tasks, our selfhood is stifled.

When methods are used that make work less meaningful, a big chunk of job value gets lopped off. Typically these procedures aim at bringing financial benefits. But whether they increase profits or not, the ultimate price is a less robust work culture. Feeling less vital, staff morale takes a hit, crashing down until slipping into a Great Depression. Opportunists, unmoved by the shift toward tension and indifference, invade. But whilst they can thrive, many people can't and are forced to leave. When dignity on the job starts eroding, work adopts a grim mood and good intentions are lost.

Working toward what we distrust is caustic. Of course many people are resigned to their situation, experiencing this feeling daily. Perhaps it is easier coping in a switched off state than feeling the dread of unemployment.

But no job *has* to be done this way.

Getting meaning from our efforts sustains our own value. That's why tasks reflecting good purpose bring fulfillment. Being involved purposefully leaves us feeling at ease and frequently offers solace.

Pairing pleasure with purpose is, therefore, more than a mere thrill. It's about creating our own satisfaction. Giving our best in that positive state has a magnifying effect. Engaged, we sense beauty. Perceiving it, we naturally want to share it.

That is why doing something that matters is vital. Pouring yourself into work you believe in enables you to reflect and experience your value.

It also helps you handle the bits you like a lot less. Focusing on higher purpose avoids becoming self-absorbed. Instead, it cultivates a greater mindfulness of *meaning* which puts unpleasant tasks into perspective. When the reason is worthy enough, likes and dislikes take a back seat and let us get more done.

"Learn to love the things you have to do," a friend of ours once explained. It was her mother's motto, many times said.

Finding ways to embrace your tasks empowers you. Not only does it make us better workers, but wanting to make a difference helps us cope. When it's tough going, it's this challenge factor that keeps drawing our attention.

The Blowtorch

No conversation about work goes too far without mentioning its pressures. Having worked in a variety of different jobs, it always comes up. After consulting with management at hundreds of workplaces as a vocational rehabilitation consultant, it's obvious. Every job has its blowtorch.

Meaning, there will always be difficulties to face. No matter how well suited to our skills and temperament the tasks are and how wonderful the workplace is, there will always be points of pressure to test your resolve.

This is why I regard workplaces as the proving grounds for personality. Whatever we do and say on the job is up front and on display for assessment and judgment.

In particular, two things keep coming up as the key areas of difficulty: relationships and the order of business.

Second-guessing intentions, experiencing frustration, and handling behavior that feels hurtful or cruel are standard fare almost everywhere. Misunderstandings are so common; we all have stories to tell.

Blustering bosses and disrespectful co-workers can make life exasperating while serving difficult customers can leave you breathlessly indignant, deeply conflicted, or both.

Listen to the water cooler conversation, and eventually there will be hushed voices. One by one people start beefing about someone or something.

Ranging from mild annoyance to serious abuse, these issues can be hard to solve. Dominating our thoughts one minute, they temporarily go to the backburner when more pressing matters appear. The standard method of handling things is burying ourselves in our work. *Put up and shut up* often makes sense. Small things pass soon enough, and even bigger things blow over eventually. But there are times when long-term resentments remain, eroding even the most supportive organization from within.

The usual way to cope is through joking as a kind of pressure relieving outlet. If this turns into ugly gossiping, it takes workplace spirit down a notch or two, which is hardly surprising. After all unresolved problems have a way of coming out in the wash, don't they?

But reaching the point where everyone is constructively talking is tricky, isn't it? Try telling your boss about his lousy manner, and you could soon be packing your desk and saying your goodbyes. Sorting out an issue of laziness with a co-worker without it causing conflict requires a tight act of diplomacy.

No wonder ignoring things is unofficially standard procedure in most workplaces. How many times have you sat tight on a work problem, hoping it would all blow over? Ignore the handbook on staff policy. This is how things happen in the real world.

If management sees the benefits of openness, they will build space for talking things through. Sometimes, if things are serious, they may even consider getting a mediator to help. Hard as it is, this can be highly constructive for what it says as much as what it does. Mediating solutions with a third party tells workers that both they and the job they perform matter.

Having been involved in mediating disputes, I believe it's a worthwhile process. Provided everyone wants a solution, going through the discomfort of sorting out problems can build trust as a welcome byproduct. Working towards mutually satisfying results validates workplace relationships and tells everyone that maturity is valued.

But if your workplace is suffering relationship tensions right now, don't hold your breath that someone will settle it by themselves. Chances are it will go under the rug with some discrete sweeping as everyone tries to get on with the job with as little conflict as possible.

By my estimate such interpersonal conflicts account for more than half of all work-related problems. The rest results from procedures.

There are systems, or a lack of them, that can drive you crazy. Like sweeping changes being implemented that will be forgotten in 3 months time. Or cringe worthy customer service spiels that even leave clients flinching. Or perhaps the disorganization that results in a complete lack of support when problems arise. These, and a thousand variations like them, make up an immense amount of workplace ugliness.

Despite even the best of intentions, some procedures can easily become intensely vexing. Meaning that workplace systems need continual checking to determine their benefit.

What can we do when these things go awry? Aside from exercising our sense of humor (a lot), we do have a few options. Firstly, identifying the extent of the problem gives us a sense of scope. Does it just frustrate you? Or does the way things get done jeopardize the harmony of the entire workplace? Are there legitimate ways of working around them for the time being? If systems are causing you serious problems, are there ways of creating better alternatives?

Having found a flaw in the system, you may be the solution everybody needs. Notwithstanding your issues, looking long term at the situation can at least put things into perspective.

If you are in a toxic workplace culture, certain symptoms will be obvious. High staff turnover, for example, suggests the blowtorch is simply too hot to handle.

If relationships are being compromised, you know something has got to give. So you can expect poor quality to appear along with a climate of strain.

Where staff members are feeling disrespected or there is an atmosphere of distrust, customers inevitably become the whipping boy. Not having to face outright anger as much as a silent emptiness, they will soon sense something isn't right.

To handle a climate of resentment, most people simply switch off. Where there is no camaraderie amongst workers or atmosphere of care and respect, work breeds a lot of ugly behavior. How often have you noticed customers being treated like objects as staff members seem to withdraw into their protective shells?

Financial ways of measuring business success are incapable of measuring relationship quality. Upfront, a clinical style might look impressive, and productivity figures could be fine. Beneath, people may be feeling nothing but apathy.

> **"Be true to your work, your word, and your friend."**
>
> Henry David Thoreau

Denying people meaningful relationships in work is not only ugly. I believe it's vastly counterproductive. Wanting more, we need to give more.

Whilst expressing *The Seven Strength*s turns down the blowtorch, their humanizing influence and quality-boosting effects also provide immense value to the workplace.

These factors mean we need to stay alert to the way we ourselves work. No matter our role, the ripple effects coming from the way we relate has knock-on effects we can direct.

If your day is being dominated by workplace hostility, you need to know *why* you're there. You also need to keep remembering the merit your presence provides.

Giving your workplace the benefit of your qualities enhances conditions at work. Functioning with beautiful purpose in mind promotes a resilience others can feel and echo for themselves. That's why operating with dignity and treating people well is part of the solution to every work-based situation.

When facing the intensity of relationship tensions and system failures, pretending things away just won't cut it. Rising above problems like infighting, power plays, and manipulation can only be done when we have solid purposes. Not just that of the workplace, but your own.

Living With Work and Family

Because work can be so all-consuming, preservation of the self is essential to living well. Whatever we do, we deserve to be working with dignity. You are not a machine of flesh. Nor are you a solitary being. Wherever you are, you deserve and need to belong. Your relationship ties are crucial to your work making sense.

Even keeping the two areas of work and home apart, there is always an emotional crossover pouring both ways. However we do it, working doesn't happen in isolation. By carefully uniting these realms together, our work can feel more purposefully humane.

Though family needs vary, having adequate personal space and privacy benefits us all.

In the media-made image, family is usually Mom, Dad, and two kids. But real families now come in all sorts of blends, don't they? Meaning families have different needs. For a long-term job to be truly satisfying, we simply cannot turn a blind eye to the demands of our particular, unique family situation.

Granted this is easier to say than do. But slowly greater flexibility *is* trickling into more jobs. Some workplaces are already incredibly accommodating to family needs. In doing so, they deserve our loyalty and custom. At the other extreme, there are still too many employers acting as if our families don't exist at all.

Work that fails to recognize your responsibilities and family priorities only increases the burden upon the worker. Rearing the next generation is, after all, no simple task. So it only makes sense that caring parents will want to do well by their children. Wise employers understand this. By striving to be family friendly, they know they will not only get greater commitment, but they promote productivity as well.

Families rearing young children certainly have an urgent need for flexibility. But without day care, negotiated hours, or at least an understanding boss, paid work hinders young families. In this all too common clash, there are no neat solutions.

So how do we make wise choices regarding our circumstances? I recommend weighing up the beauty behind your own values. Let what *you* passionately believe be your guide. Give preference to what matters in the long term.

Though parenting is the basis of every successful society, we all know it certainly doesn't pay bills. Nor does it offer the opportunities of a career. Yet the importance of your unpaid role as a parent cannot be overstated. The future depends on it.

Balancing the needs of children with work is tough, and I suspect most men aren't close enough to the action to appreciate this. Juggling a job and family takes dual focus, practice, and wise compromise. All of which get much harder when fatigue or illness enter the equation.

Whatever our work demands, children need someone on hand, don't they? Somebody showing them practical love and affection is the core of parenthood.

No matter how we try structuring it, young children's need for nurture is enormous. The best measurement I can think of is that it feels greater than you can give. So with both parenting and work being so open-ended, each keeps vying for time and headspace.

This perpetual conflict partly explains the terrible guilt so many working mothers feel. Teaching young children has raised my consciousness of how burdened and anxious many mothers are. What they are missing is the recognition that they are doing the best they can. Struggling to keep it all together, most say combining paid work and parenting leaves them feeling terribly guilty and utterly exhausted.

Given just how much most women manage to achieve in a day, I believe this guilt generally comes from trying to achieve impossibly high goals. That's not going to comfort anyone. But it's good to get perspective. With two, and frequently even more, competing demands, being a working mother is bound to be frustratingly difficult.

When Ruth was pregnant with our boys, she kept working right up until they were born. With Ben she went into labor within hours of working late.

Then, whilst they were babies, Ruth worked as much as she could and still managed to breastfeed and care for them both. By the time our children were toddlers, we co-parented, mixing in some day care to help. It worked well. But that didn't stop Ruth feeling that, somehow, she could have or *should* have done a better job.

Which is a telling thing because, however you choose to do it, you will probably feel guilty too. With infinite room for thinking you aren't doing enough, many mothers suffer ongoing attacks of self-blame.

My response is to say there is no world authority with an easy solution for your family-work situation. Finding your own way that works is actually the best it gets.

Mercifully, kids are incredibly resilient. So long as they know they are loved, get enough sleep, good nutrition, and play, they can flourish quite happily.

Still, things would be better if parents had more support. Getting help is the puzzle piece so often missing in modern life. It makes so much sense, I believe, that it's worth factoring in as a key priority when choosing where to live. Having your extended family and other trustworthy people to share the care is a win for everyone, including your children. Most importantly, it helps you cope. Yet often it seems to be put down the list beneath a checklist of other benefits like a bigger house or nicer neighborhood.

This much is obvious: rearing kids is one of the biggest things we will ever do. Its consequences are unknowably far-reaching, as any great-grandparent knows. So, like anything major, it's challenging. Combining parenting and working takes monumental organization, *heart*, and *fortitude*. So developing a caring network is a great investment in the practical art of making your life more beautiful.

Connecting with other families going through the same challenges can also be a wonderfully bonding experience. Aside from moral support, working families can share babysitting, cleaning, shopping, or almost anything that helps balance the load. Forging helpful partnerships may be driven by convenience, but the byproduct of building good relationships during an otherwise hectic and disconnecting time in life is satisfaction in itself.

The pressure of time and trouble managing are reminders of how we can help others too. When we are also busy that might sound ridiculous. But busy people are the ones who most often get things done, don't they? Besides, knowing what people are going through means we can be a true support for them.

Gifting time to help when people are struggling is a down to earth expression of *heart* and *wisdom*. Persevering through tiredness with *fortitude*, we can speak the language of beauty clearly and simply through our actions.

Position, Position, Position

What do property agents know about working beautifully? The answer is position. Not in terms of property investment but belonging. How far you end up travelling to and from your workplace helps set the scene. Why? Because your life is always going to be influenced by the time and quality of your commuting experience.

With ever-increasing commuting distances and suburbia growing, our home time together is shrinking. For many, hardly anything is within easy walking distance. Instead, we've accepted that distance is irrelevant if it's only a drive away.

So if you're working in paid employment, how far do you travel to get to work? Half an hour? An hour or maybe two? Perhaps it feels like your commute is getting too much for you.

Finding more affordable housing further out and wanting a higher standard of living are key factors driving increased travel. Thanks to good cars and better transport networks, we can do it. But the benefits come at a high cost. Spending more of our time just getting where we want to be is ramping up the pressure. With the convenience of the Internet and cell phones, we've forgotten how much wear and tear there is in real world travel.

Being stuck in tediously long commutes means more than just missing a bit of extra sleep. Spending too long in transit is diluting our influence. Yet squandering time in endless processions of traffic is more than tolerated. It's a badge of honor, giving us boasting rights. How many traffic jam stories have you heard told at the water cooler?

Trading time for more space, we keep travelling further for longer. Yet, so long as it's popularly accepted, going back and forth daily doesn't seem such a sacrifice. Besides, we can always occupy ourselves purposely on the way.

Still, longer and longer trips are becoming a dominating influence. How many dads, for instance, spend more time commuting than with their children? What are we losing in exchange?

Okay, I'm nailing my colors to the mast. I believe commuting daily for long periods is generally a poor choice with serious side effects on your family and self. Repeatedly going into a holding pattern that's neither here nor there is robbing people of precious interpersonal contact.

Fighting through long lines of traffic to get to work won't earn anyone's appreciation. Battling for hours in traffic or casually arriving after a twenty-minute strolling commute, theoretically, has no bearing on work. But it can have a dramatic impact on you.

Having a beautiful life now is not about having it all. Nor is it necessarily about shaving a few extra minutes off the trip to work. It's applying *wisdom* and *honesty* to our situations so we don't forfeit our personal satisfaction for something that reduces our meaning in life.

> "But better die than live mechanically a life that is a repetition of repetitions."
>
> D. H. Lawrence

In my twenties, I turned my interest in photography into a job. Working in a photographic store across town meant travelling two and a half hours each way. That's no big deal. But sitting in my little blue *Datsun*, stuck behind fuming lines of vehicles, I began realizing how pointless it was. With none of us wanting to be there, we were wasting our lives. Together in our shiny metal boxes, we were surrounded yet totally alone.

Plenty of us use our commute for phone calls, relaxing, or reading. There are lots of ways to get something out of what would otherwise be wasted time. But if you can do it, try making your commuting time brief. You will have greater choices, more time with the people you care about, and extra opportunities for hobbies and health.

To me, long distance commuting is only part of a trend toward communities fragmenting. With forty million Americans moving annually and three-fourths of the entire population moving every five years, no wonder it's hard to establish deep community connections.

> "Better do a good deed near at home than go far away to burn incense."
>
> Amelia Earhart

Finding a place that ties work with home is about bucking that trend and finding more satisfaction. Imagine getting to know people more deeply because you've known them for years. Perhaps even have your extended family close by.

Concentrating on bricks and mortar amenities at the expense of our lifelong needs for social amenity is isolating us. No matter how good things can be, there is no substitute for long-term relationships.

Not surprisingly, choosing to be closer to work, school, and family can be a complex affair. More than likely there will be tradeoffs, especially if you have a partner working twenty miles in the opposite direction. Or the schools you prefer are nowhere nearby. Not to mention the difficulty of affording property close by.

Your planning, therefore, should aim for durable solutions, taking everything you can into account (perhaps even your next job change). In deciding, give relationships priority. Consider which combination gives you the best sense of connection all round.

With cities continually growing, the tendency for more urban sprawl remains. How tempting then to move just a few more miles out, enjoying a bigger place for less? That's why we need to keep reminding ourselves just what's at stake.

> **"Where we love is home. Home that our feet may leave, but not our hearts."**
>
> Oliver Wendell Holmes

Being further from family and friends naturally leads to seeing less of each other. So countering the isolation requires us to actively get involved in local life. Unfortunately, social networks and belonging take time to develop. Being busy and mostly away at work, forming new friendships is often as challenging as it is slow going. On top of that, growing good relationships takes time anyway. Fast friendships, like fast food, are all too easily disposable.

When home and work are close, our sense of local connection almost grows by itself. Being there, we are part of the community. Day and night. Rushing less, we can belong more.

When our kids can see where we work, they also appreciate the connection. Shopping locally, we work out who's who in the neighborhood. Getting together with friends we can talk, play, reminisce, and feel a sense of belonging. Having work and relationships closer to hand we can experience the simple beauty of being at home in community.

Working Spirit

Connectedness like this builds an enduring working spirit. Whether close to home, together with workmates, or forging relationships with customers, our efforts flourish with human contact.

Bringing your own version of *The Seven Strengths* to work puts the emphasis on quality. Reflecting beauty in your work habits and relationships naturally feeds back into your attitude. Instead of regard being a polite veneer of surface support, we take our integrity with us. Not to steer each conversation to some meaningfully deep purpose or to adopt the role of chief problem-sharing groupie. But to be genuine, diligent, and receiving of others with sincerity.

Sharing the best we have to offer can be as quiet or upfront as we choose. What matters is that we keep applying the qualities of beauty to our situation in ways we can believe in. That's necessary because work has a way of challenging our attitudes.

Skin-deep effort and simple pleasantries offer short-lived results and can undermine our own working spirit. That's why honesty about what matters to us should be the basis of our commitment. How much drive we want our work to express really comes down to meaning, not willpower.

> **"Dare to be honest and fear no labor."**
> Robert Burns

Working with commitment, we deserve to be proud about our work efforts. Basing dedication on our own standards rather than merely trying to please is a statement of personal quality. Regardless of what's happening at work, our working spirit has little to do with the boss and everything to do with us.

Should we choose, we can be an asset to the business. We can under promise and over deliver, raising the bar to our own higher level. Just as we can create a better environment by being true to our word. In a world of plastic promises, it takes more than fast talking lip service. Instead, building a reputation from our own standards

> *"Work hard and become a leader; be lazy and never succeed."*
>
> Proverbs 12:24

reveals our principles as our chief asset. With them we can go far beyond position, obligations, or payment.

Revealing the quality of our character, personal principles should never be up for auction. Giving you reasons to stand by co-workers, company, or customers, they are the foundations strengthening your working spirit. When things go wrong, they give you the dignity to accept mistakes and find solutions. Your standards are your hallmark.

Naturally, practically everyone starts a new job with good intentions. Teachable and willing, people are too busy learning to do anything but do the job well. Then, over time, there's a slide. A case of listening less and presuming more. Humility disappears as superiority takes place.

That's where *The Seven Strengths* stand out, giving us reason to receive new ideas and fresh possibilities. Even if our boss lacks leadership, we can continue demonstrating the dignity of our character. Regardless of whether resentments are justified, our integrity stands steadfastly above it all.

Enduring qualities have the greatest impact. Major difficulties may leave us feeling we need to flee, deny, or fight. But having beautiful ways to respond gives us the basis to stand firm and apply ourselves.

Consider *giving, fortitude, honesty, heart, releasing, visioning*, and *wisdom* as essential tools. Tackling different work situations requires their use in different combinations. Having different pathways of expression with them, you have much more than a "can do" attitude to offer. You have a context to define your actions. Being disciplined or happily enthusiastic is great, but they come nowhere near for lasting effect. With beautiful strengths you have far more than pep talk to inspire others. You have the power to create and encourage with a lasting legacy.

Your efforts have a compounding effect as people begin realizing who you are and how you work. Having a working spirit that considers the welfare of others is automatically inclusive. Knowing nothing great can be achieved with selfishness, short term thinking, or deception, you naturally think bigger and better.

Being a go-getter in itself is marvelous but not enough if we want to live a beautiful life. Achieving needs dignity to give it lasting quality. Picking up the pieces left by so many wheeler-dealers, isn't it time we raise the caliber of our work to a new standard? One that principled people can hold in high regard and set as a benchmark.

Working with a spirit of beauty rests upon a desire to do better with character. Occasionally it means doing some mental gymnastics to sense the importance of cleaning the toilets and mopping the floors. But it's worth it. Turning all the little things into meaningful moments converts chore-filled time into consequential living. By consciously focusing, we inhabit the here-and-now to the fullest degree.

Things like unexpectedly helping workmates meet a deadline or tidying up someone else's mess may be minor, but they make a difference. Building our self-approval on the solid ground of worthy action is satisfying in itself. Speaking up for others is affirming whether it's noticed or not. Finding more effective ways to do a job always matters, regardless of who notices. The point is, *you notice*. Because we always remember the worthiness of our own deeds, that counts most.

Inhabiting your work world with a commitment to quality is a compelling statement of self-expression. You don't do it for the money alone. You do it to reflect and fulfill your identity.

Whether creating new approaches, helping customers, sorting problems, or doing backroom stuff, your identity comes out. Being involved perfectly positions you to present your best. Not all the time, but over time.

So, I say, whether it's work for pay or work for love, commit yourself to be a pleasing influence. Let everything you care about have the touch of your hand upon it.

Chapter 10

Growing Relationships

"Happiness is having a large, loving, caring, close-knit family in another city."

George Burns

Character Is King

Have you noticed how frequently beauty in relationships drops off the radar in modern life? Despite a growing need for *heart* in personal and public life, a blind spot is forming. Expressing tenderness and love are increasingly seen as *soft* or *awkward*. Increasingly, relationship beauty is being considered as *quaint*.

To live a full life, your relationships need to be healthy too. Like the people you remember who put beauty into your childhood through surprising kindness, loyalty, or sacrifice, they taught you something about social wellbeing.

Now, having been woven into your life, those past experiences of beauty are still shaping your values. Far from being temporary, our healthy sense of self rests on the beauty we've known. Continuously feeding our inspiration, it also keeps determining the quality of our connection with others.

Sharing beauty in your relationships is nurturing for everyone. What friendship doesn't need *heart* to bring comfort? Or *wisdom* and *honesty* to weather the storms? Investing *The Seven Strengths* in our relationships promotes deeper beauty and fuller happiness. With

> "No act of kindness, no matter how small, is ever wasted."
>
> Aesop, "The Lion and the Mouse"

them, friendships can flourish where they otherwise might flounder.

Being so aware of these qualities, you see beauty where others may only see difficulty. When a friend opens up to you, revealing her pain. Or when a family, having lost a loved one to crime, publicly forgives the perpetrator. There amidst the pain, they are choosing *honesty, fortitude*, and *release*. Beauty like this can pierce the hardest armor. When it hits you, the effect is profound.

It amazes me that anyone could regard expressing tenderness as weak. But an uncaring few do. They prefer idolizing hardened heroes, admiring them for their robust toughness. Hero worship is fine, but the hardiness they admire needs to go down deeper than force. To me, true strength is about the courage to do what we believe in. To stand by somebody when they need you or have the courage to demonstrate vulnerability takes incredible spirit. That's something no amount of domination can produce. What's more, it takes *heart* and *wisdom* to do it.

> "Compassion is the basis of all morality."
>
> Arthur Schopenhauer

True character, I believe, is always about going beyond comfort to do something important. With *fortitude*, even the frailest, most timid person can demonstrate immense character. The secret lies in the resolve we apply.

By contrast aggressive chest beating certainly looks powerful and gets attention. But to me it's just excess testosterone minus the mindfulness. Unless tied to qualities of character, what passes for might is merely brute force, whether good or bad.

Giving your best to your relationships is not idealistic. More a case of living true to yourself. Your highest values need expressing. Not least because that is the most unselfish way of showing you count.

Facing Family

What makes family important? And how do you feel about your own? Contrary to all the schmaltzy greeting card sentiments, family attracts a much wider range of feelings than they would be willing to print. That's because family life can be supremely joyful or fiercely difficult. Close or distant, your family nonetheless gives you the ultimate place for growing. So it stands that we are constantly being both drawn and repelled by our family relationships.

> *"Act with kindness, but do not expect gratitude."*
> Confucius

As a source of immense comfort and pleasure, there is little to compare with a happy family environment. When it functions well, there is a richness of relationship that puts each piece of the happiness puzzle into place. Small or large, immediate or extended, family gives us our beginnings. Due to its intensity, family has an incredible impact on our lives. That's why delving into your family experience is so revealing about the way you think, live, and love. With its ups and downs, family provides the footing for making sense of this world. It is our primary line of empowerment and a source of deep belief.

> *"Honesty is the first chapter in the book of wisdom."*
> Thomas Jefferson

Yet often growing up and forming relationships are areas fraught with confusion and worry. Misunderstandings and hurts can all-too-easily accumulate. Silently entwining into tangled resentments, family problems can trip us up. Despite the best of intentions, they can leave family relationships tarnished.

Behind the posed smiles of each family portrait lies a hidden realm, which even the happiest families have. Here things can lie dormant, unresolved for years where the distress and disappointments of daily history are tossed out of sight.

What can we do to tend our own collection of hurts? As I see it, a good head for forgetting slights and snarling comes in handy. Best to forget than remain stuck in the cycle of blaming. But if you can't, bravely and kindly expressing your views sets the scene. Start with an issue that keeps building up. Problems swept out of sight under pressure have to be faced at some stage, don't they? Stating your concerns at least begins the conversation. You have to start somewhere.

With pain comes reaction, so *honesty* often meets distress. Talk over your feelings using every one of *The Seven Strengths* as touchstones. Knowing how moods change, you cannot guarantee how it will be received. But at least you can set the tone by communicating with dignity.

Naturally, this is just the beginning. Making happy endings out of family feuds only happens reliably in TV situation dramas (typically about five minutes before the credits roll). Speaking up is like scratching flint, sparks often lead to ignition. Moreover, people want to keep doing what they want. So a toddler or a teen will not be inclined to cooperate unless there's a mighty good reward in it for them.

But it can get more complicated than that. If your father was a drunken abuser, your enlightened approach is hardly going to be his idea of improvement. Never mind that even wanting relationship with him might be the last thing you want to face.

Then there are whole families rife with cruelty and violence toward each other. Getting involved, even just to talk, can be toxic, if not downright dangerous.

Transforming a clan is rarely in one person's hands. So a practical approach might be extending our sense of family with people who are more whole and balanced.

In the end changing our family's ways may not be as crucial as refashioning our own. Managing the misunderstandings, hurt, and hostility we experience has two important effects.

Firstly, we learn to cope. Finding sense in ourselves, we increasingly find freedom from the frustration. That gives us healing space.

Secondly, our life spills over, registering in our family's awareness. They can, of course, choose to ignore you. But the impact of you

> "Wishing to be friends is quick work, but friendship is a slow ripening fruit."
>
> Aristotle

kindling beauty is there all the same, showing them another path. Maybe that's all you need to do.

To my mind, it sure beats the alternative of pretending all is sweetness and light when it's not. Wanting neat relationship is more about the need for control than desiring to engage deeply. In many ways, "neat" and "deep" are polar opposites. Wanting it all spic-and-span signals something disquieting. Think of the couples you see on TV who, even after fifty years of marriage, boast they've never had a spat. What haven't they been talking about to avoid that?

When people say their marriage "needs work," I believe they're really saying there's little sign of *The Seven Strengths* in their relationship. For marriage to feel like an empty shell, it's the beauty that is missing.

You might wonder how any of us can get to that stage. I suspect it comes from skipping the difficulties confronting our weaknesses cause. Preferring the more appealing theme of happiness with no end, we naturally avoid the tricky bits. This is where blockages begin and why flushing out the buildup of relationship gunk that blocks our communicative arteries is so vital.

> "No legacy is so rich as honesty."
>
> William Shakespeare

Couples unwilling to get their hands dirty are going to find fulfillment fleeting. That's because removing ugly resentments, fears, and selfishness will always prove a messy endeavor. Fortunately, in the discomfort of this awkward process, we not only grow together, but we grow up.

The same goes when we're rearing children. Starting out, who can imagine how complicated and challenging it will be? Caught up in the constancy of parenting, the beauty of each moment can skip right past us, leaving us wondering where it all went.

Making do and feeling inadequate, our parenting journey can be more like staggering than strolling. Thankfully, since nobody agrees

> *"We never know the love of our parents for us till we have become parents."*
>
> Henry Ward Beecher

on the standards, there isn't an ideal version of parenting. Instead, there are many.

Whichever way, kids need us to live out *The Seven Strengths* like they need sunshine, sleep, and play. Having an inborn compass for beauty, young children are naturally drawn to it. Thriving on expressions of *heart*, children also crave our *honesty*. Our love is their shelter and inspiration.

We can give our kids many things, many of which don't last the distance. Inevitably, knick-knacks are not enough to build them up. But giving children our version of *The Seven Strengths* is totally different. Instead of dispensing trinkets, we share our treasure.

To me family is a defining feature of life. Whether we spend an entire life desperately running from them or simply standing by them, family inevitably remains. As our most intimate form of community, family is our main proving ground, a place of rigorous testing for our character and the ultimate test of our beauty.

For a Grand Love – Refuge of the Heart

For all the talk about how to live our love life, there seems to be precious little about relationship sustainability. Yet getting bogged down by all of the problems and distractions of life is an all too common challenge. According to men I've met seeking new relationships, routines and sameness cause a sharp decline in intimacy. That's why they walked out on their partners. Finding their love lives lacking, they confided they were now looking elsewhere for closeness and sexual fulfillment.

There is something odd about this reaction, isn't there? Hoping for more, all these guys can possibly achieve is perhaps yet another version of the same. To me, their diagnosis of the problem is painfully lacking in insight. The difficulty has more to do with them not fully grasping what being a loving partner is about.

A lover is not merely someone smitten. That's a lovesick admirer.

Loving partners are bound to each other with the privilege of a deep and abiding intimacy. With the ability to give each other something no one else can provide, they offer deep refuge. A sense of place where the very essence of that person can feel safe, appreciated, and supported. Don't we all need that? More than anything else, the greatest purpose for each lover is to provide a safe haven of love.

> *"There is no more lovely, friendly and charming relationship, communion or company than a good marriage."*
>
> Martin Luther

Given our uniqueness as individuals, this place is shaped by every person's deepest needs. If your loved one craves stability and peace more than anything else, then you shape your life to make that happen for him or her at all costs. Maybe she longs to be filling her days with fantasy and fun. Or maybe he has an abiding delight that captivates his attention. Whatever your partner's enduring desires, accepting that yearning supports your relationship intimacy and, ultimately, nurtures *your* happiness.

Can you have a *reasonable* life together ignoring this? I imagine so. But never a grand love. By supporting your partner's passions, you affirm them being themselves. Where your partner's needs have meaning and respect, you are helping intimacy to thrive. When togetherness has meaning beyond the traditions of routines and responsibilities, you are forging a marriage of souls. For as long as each partner lives with this understanding, the pressures of ordinary life and growing old cannot undo their attraction.

To me, intimacy that gives so wholly is continually attractive. Distractions come and go. But, I believe, we are all drawn to someone who understands our deepest longings and welcome them as part of us.

With *gemütlichkeit*, we know how to do this well. Away from work, even in precious minutes alone together, we can anchor our partner to the here and now. Not blurting out thoughts about responsibilities and permitting silence is a deliberately soothing gesture. Temporarily putting aside our own worries and problems, we can consciously but casually aim to put our partner at ease. By freeing them, we free

> *"Guard well within yourself that treasure, kindness. Know how to give without hesitation, how to lose without regret, how to acquire without meanness."*
>
> George Sand

ourselves. Creating simple moments like this, couples can switch off the distraction and build closeness. For a partner craving order and stability, for instance, making the background effort of cleaning might do the same thing. Or perhaps paying bills or providing a meal when you feel too tired.

"Give them what they long for," Martha advised me. Long widowed when I met her, she was an old woman with a young mind, brimming with wisdom. Her words keep rolling around my thoughts to this day. By respecting your partner's needs, you insulate the bonds of love between you. So when a partner shapes his day with the purpose of appreciating your inner needs, it's a sign of his grand passion.

Is it easy to love so fully? Only if our path is clear. Making a haven for your partner takes active and conscious effort to beat distraction, discomfort, and tiredness. However, these actions are not the work of a martyr. That would undermine everything. Developing our skills to make a place for our lover's longings is simply an act of beauty. Like a work of fine art, it is valued most by those who appreciate their life lived at full strength.

Couples wanting a grand love to last a lifetime still face the same undermining challenges. Even the most ardent couple cannot stop the effects of family quarrels, aging, and work hassles. But finding the key to keeping us committed to each other is a beautiful, life-changing discovery. One that goes beyond duty, promises, and whims. Practical day-to-day effort that cares for our partner in ways they value affirms our closeness to each other. But it is possible to go even further by placing a partner's needs within the core of our very life purpose. That is the mark of a true lover.

Enriching as it is, a grand love needs more than passion. Achieving it requires combined *honesty* too. Discerning what our lover longs for is not always obvious. For this reason, knowing the difference between longing and selfishness takes *wisdom*. Sometimes what

> *"An honest answer is the sign of true friendship."*
> Proverbs 24:26

drives us is rooted in anxiety, and lovers need to sensitively uncover their motivations. Just as there needs to be an abiding respect for each other's uniqueness, valuing your differences celebrates each other.

Forging a great love is a two-way affair in which degrees of giving will vary. But an abiding togetherness carries the safety of confidence. The key is to continue being open to each other with precious honesty to strengthen that trust.

Expressing the great qualities of beauty in our love creates something more than a satisfying relationship. It inspires joy and mutual admiration. Unsurprisingly, others can feel it coming from your relationship too. But what is most remarkable is how much a grand love *encourages* others. Finding fulfillment in your togetherness is something children can inherit and even communities can look up to. Creating a haven of love may even be one of the most beautiful contributions we will ever make.

Holding on Gently

Yet we know love rarely follows an even course. There are low times in every great relationship when you just need to keep hanging in there. Not desperately clutching on in fear, but gently holding onto what you believe is meaningful in your togetherness.

When the embers start fading in your relationship, realize that this is no failing but a natural progression. Expecting love to unfold smoothly year-by-year is unrealistic. Challenges and stages are normal and even worthwhile. Far from failure, they may be necessary aids to help you grow together. True, problems in relationship are potential flash points. But they are also opportunities to break new ground.

When I think back over the past thirty years with Ruth, I know our hard times have been where we've done the most growing. Each has been a rude shock, forcing us to think differently and adapt. We've had to hang on at times with sheer *fortitude*, riding out the hurt, just as we needed to keep finding new ways to love.

> "Where there's marriage without love, there will be love without marriage."
>
> Benjamin Franklin

Knowing each other intimately is its own reward, yet it also opens the door to new levels. There you begin to see the problems that you, as a couple, are yet to resolve. Keeping them in the denial basket just won't work. Suppressing and keeping secrets won't wash. Like hiding hurts, they reflect a refusal to develop. Moving on means one of you, at least, needs to be expressing qualities of beauty.

When there has been a lot of relationship drift, our certainties begin diminishing. As a result you might get the feeling that you don't love your partner anymore. That is so incredibly confronting that I suspect a lot of couples simply try burying it. Out of mind but never fully out of sight, it festers like a sore. Yet facing this hurdle is an important step on the path to sharing a deeper, more satisfying relationship.

Quitting, on the other hand, prevents us from ever knowing better. But going through the motions, hoping habit force will fix everything doesn't work either. We've tried that a number of times. But the holding pattern only puts you on a slow decline into despair.

I suspect the uniqueness we fall for in each other when we first meet sparks healthy admiration and flexibility. But being besotted, we soon become entwined. Gradually adopting each other's ways, we willingly blur our behaviors, and our selves, together. We like it. But by taking the path of identity-loss, our distinctiveness loses its gloss. Becoming one runs the risk that we can end up missing each other. No longer two separate lovers reveling in each other's uniqueness, we become a mini-franchise with two managers in charge wearing the same uniform.

Nobody dreams of becoming a blended blob with the love of their life. Nor does it feature as a possible hazard on the horizon. So when it happens, I've observed couples doing different things to compensate. Like clinging desperately to happier times. Perhaps surrendering past excitement for a future of boredom spanning as far as the eye can see. Or, starting to actively despise one another for what the other has become.

Blurring our unique selves can make us want to push each other away. Like relationships pulling apart for lack of enough in common, the results are similar. If we are unable to diagnose the cause, a sad finale is a real possibility.

Prolonged unhappiness becomes proof that a relationship is failing and, therefore, cannot be fixed. I'm oversimplifying about these matters, so I apologize if your circumstances are different. But don't we tend to trust our long-term feelings?

We enter long-term relationships believing they will last. So it's unlikely we will be preventing problems we don't expect. Instead, it's as if they just happen. Then, if we believe picking up the shards isn't worth the pain, the cast is set.

> "Love always brings difficulties, that is true, but the good side of it is that it gives energy."
>
> Vincent van Gogh

If happily ever after was all we had to cling to on our relationship journey then I imagine even our lifeboat would spring a leak.

But what if we knew *The Seven Strengths* were the building blocks of satisfying relationship? Like all the other obstacles, losing sight of our individuality would then be seen as something to grow through.

Whenever we are being problem-focused, we are likely to dismiss the influence of *qualities* as barriers to our *wants*. But the merits of beauty are enduring. We can hold onto them whenever life gets tough. Relationship problems will always be the intense kind of learning experiences we never want to face. But because dealing with them is inevitable, you can't purely rely on hoping. Holding adamantly to your values and relying on *The Seven Strengths* gives you a far better way to cope with these hurdles.

With *heart, fortitude*, and a generous sprinkling of *wisdom*, it is possible to build a new life. But if you want more, you will need to give and communicate more deeply to achieve it.

Reaffirming your love requires talking through your awareness, fears, and needs. Escaping from "assumption land," we can begin questioning our habits. Discovering yourself like this in relationship means accepting that perhaps a bit of anything really is possible. By holding on gently, we can re-energize attraction, making room for the originality we always admired.

Nourishing Intimacy with Others

Closeness expresses its quality in relationship beauty far beyond sexual encounters. Courage and openness are cherished in every good relationship. That willingness to let yourself reach into the realm of another soul bridges our separation. In the shared moment, revealing your feelings about anything becomes an intimate experience. Sharing a secret. Appreciating a word, thought, or gesture from another. Being aware enough to delight in the presence of someone we care about. Creating a conversation of togetherness. These shared experiences are the lifeblood of intimacy.

> *"It is one of the blessings of old friends that you can afford to be stupid with them."*
>
> Ralph Waldo Emerson

For something that seems so personal and inward, intimacy takes a surprising amount of reaching out away from you. Being close demands awareness beyond ourselves. Discovering what someone truly cherishes takes us past the obvious. Receiving *live*, not second-guessing.

Expressing true feelings means being vulnerable. Pressured to impress, admitting simple joys can feel more like confessing. But learning where someone's happiness lies and respecting his or her likes is beautifully affirming. In every relationship trusting relies on the strength of our confidences. They are the moments of openness that we cling to and reward with loyalty.

Such true-heartedness often begins in simple kindness, doesn't it? Remember your delight over a small indulgence that was given to you with care? Your pleasure in that event is the clue to making intimate moments happen for others too.

Not that it's cupcakes, cards, tickets, or flowers alone that please. Nor the countless other generosities we can give. It's that someone is thinking enough to care. Sharing slices of chocolate cake, precious keepsakes, or delicious moments of freedom are gestures of heart. Going out of her way to share, the giver creates a delicious moment. Continuing, she builds togetherness.

> *"Life is short, but there is always time enough for courtesy."*
> Ralph Waldo Emerson

Ruth is a dab hand at turning simple moments into special events. She does it naturally. My efforts are more labored, needing me to think them through to make them happen. But I have friends who have no idea how to nourish intimacy. For them, it's a matter of waiting for that ideal moment that, as it happens, never actually comes.

Hoping to be in right time and place, some regard intimacy as lucky chemistry. Stumbling upon it is marvelous. But it's a rare element. Surrounded by people all needing closeness, it's amazing there's so precious little to be had. The scarcity will continue unless *we* create the opportunities to make closeness ourselves.

Whether it comes easily or takes much crafting, the qualities of *visioning* and *giving* are good for every relationship. Being more appreciative, some people will warmly receive and share in turn. Some, as we know too well, won't budge an inch. Focusing everywhere else, they are too removed from relationship to notice anything beyond themselves. Or, the opposite. Mistaking intentions, they translate kind gestures in ways we wouldn't dream of.

Aren't these the rules of engagement we learn by trial and error? The more personal and intense, the more risky. That's the story of intimacy. Risking much, we give of ourselves, to encourage someone else to reach out too.

Nourishing intimacy is a form of *kindling* that relies on *The Seven Strengths* to express it best. Celebrating appreciation, it defines our desire for togetherness with quality. Conveying our good intentions to others, we are also affirming ourselves with the value of *giving, honesty,* and *heart*.

Sharing intimacy requires *wisdom* above all because closeness can easily corrupt. Even innocent moments of intimacy can be craftily exploited with a Judas kiss. Just as emotional intensity can swamp our integrity, so closeness concentrates the nature of relationship. With discerning eyes, we do well to protect the pleasure of togetherness and preserve it from deceit.

Eyeballing the Armor

Speaking of being aware, I have a question for you. Did you notice you put on your armor this morning? Having donned it daily for all these years, I expect you didn't. Being so familiar, I expect it's one of those comfortably reassuring things to do.

Protecting our vulnerability, our hard casing mostly stays hidden beneath a friendlier exterior. Wearing it is more as a "just in case" thing. Not that we count on using it often, we keep it on to avoid getting hurt. So it's mostly concealed.

Noticing the armor of others is far more likely to grab our attention than discovering our own. Revealing it to repel relationship is their way of saying *"Get back!"* or *"Keep away from me."* Such awkward, clanking displays are a bit embarrassing. So we're likely to find them disturbing, explaining why we don't like to talk about this armor stuff too much.

There are a multitude of disguises too. Some are more obvious while others are well concealed. Take the critical comedian who uses laughs to pick on people. Getting everyone laughing at the vulnerabilities of others hits a twitchy nerve. One where laughing comes as much from embarrassment as from humor. Feeling open to being humiliated, attempts at *honesty* or closeness are stifled. So whilst everybody is laughing along, the crowd reassuringly clutch onto their armor. Just in case. There can't be any harm in that, right?

What about the stunningly attractive celebrities? Dazzling you with their sense of style and elegance, their appearance impresses to the point of

> "Sincerity is an openness of heart; we find it in very few people; what we usually see is only an artful dissimulation to win the confidence of others."
>
> François de la Rochefoucauld

being daunting. You might feel personally reaching out to them would be impossible. Transformed into an idol, they become trapped by their self-imposed superiority.

Then there are the powerful executives. Exuding confidence, they present themselves as the full package. Highly organized and self-disciplined, they exude authority. Speaking to them about their personal fears and hopes seems silly. Relationship has to stay at arm's length, and nobody even questions the armor.

Whenever relating to people feels embarrassing, it's likely that person's protective layer is doing its job, and it's doing it well.

So you might be wondering, *"So what? I don't need to get up close and personal with everybody. In fact I'm used to things the way they are."*

Whilst it's true wearing relationship armor serves a purpose, often to do with status, becoming aware of it is important. Consciously noticing the ways we protect and deflect in daily relationship awakens us to a host of hidden agendas. Getting to the bottom of them gives us more resilience than armor could ever grant. With the freedom of *wisdom*, we can even remove our defenses, discovering a totally new experience of connection and shared experience.

Why would we want to do that? Well, there's a price paid for wearing this heavy gear. Being on guard to protect our fragile sense of self keeps us on the back foot. Working at looking good all the time or staying in character is draining. Plus, as much as we succeed in keeping threat out, we lock ourselves in, imprisoning the self behind cold, emotionless steel.

Becoming your best self naturally means opening new pathways for expression. Flinging off restricting effects can seem strange. But isn't the comfort of simply being yourself remarkably satisfying?

No longer needing to prove your good self allows people to access to the realest form of you. It's a reasonable idea in principle. But actually allowing people to get close enough to see you as you are can be anxiety provoking. Dropping our armor is a big thing.

Recognizing the ways we block others is the first step. Believing things like *"I have to keep impressing people"; "I need to win people's sympathies"* or, *"I have to sense people's approval for me to feel okay"* might seem benign. But as much as they are about getting, they are also all about defending.

Constantly needing to excessively impress makes intimacy too risky. So when failure is prohibited, adopting a false image is just our way of coping. Needing approval insists on controlling closeness. Demanding safety over *honesty* requires strict conditions. When it's severe enough, this can have a distorting effect on relationships. From smothering to icily controlling, people will do almost anything to avoid facing social pain.

> **"No legacy is so rich as honesty."**
> William Shakespeare

Closeness doesn't immediately spring from an authentic life. But it helps. There is something deeply comforting about people being okay with themselves. Look at the most popular "ordinary" people you know, and you'll see they don't seem to have much armor. Despite the obvious risks of hurt, letting people see us "warts and all" is healthy, courageous, and inspiring. Giving them the opportunity to love and fully accept us for being real is a worthy reward.

Consider it a step toward greater satisfaction and togetherness with the people we appreciate. Being ourselves with those closest to us builds that crucial sense of togetherness we crave. With profound reassurance, true friends prove the virtue of being down-to-earth.

Stripping off the defensive armor allows you to delight in the bounty of having more of such heartfelt friendships. But whether it's approved of or not, daring to be your true self is the first step on the road to happiness.

Finding your own meaning from what you personally believe gives you the promise of fulfillment. While discovering the power of the great strengths of life builds your beauty in the purest form. These are the refreshing signs of an abundantly beautiful life. One that only *you* can live.

A Final Word to You

If you have been inspired to live more of your best self and want to share your personal experiences with others, www.happy.fm is a good place to start. With information and advice, you can tap into a wealth of useful support from people around the world.

As the Swedish proverb says, *"Shared joy is a double joy; shared sorrow is half sorrow."* So I invite you to make yourself known, join with others, and continue discovering your beauty.

Looking forward to getting to know you,

Christian (Feegs)

Appendix

How do you go about discovering your beauty?

Beauty is something we all want. Though discerned differently by everyone, we all experience it.

Today the type of beauty that's heavily promoted is based on appearance. And it's getting narrower and increasingly unobtainable. The reason? Beauty is now seen largely as a commercial product. To have it we feel we need to *buy* it.

Causing as much, if not more, despair as it does happiness, this treatment is harming us all.

A Refreshing Alternative

You know this, but your views are being suppressed: beauty stands for much more than looks. It covers a vast array of things that we appreciate; all of which bring delight and satisfaction.

That's why there's something missing. Today beauty is portrayed as a one-way experience, but it need not be this way. Your part in *recognizing* beauty is vital to releasing it.

Given your role in creating beauty, everything that would be beautiful can only be released by beholding. You have this essential ability. In its own way, it gives you influence.

To some degree we each possess two talents for experiencing beauty. I call them *revering* and *kindling*.

- *Revering* is your way of discerning beauty and appreciating its influence.
- *Kindling* goes the next step as you create beauty through intentions and actions.

Just as you are capable of causing harm, so you also have the power to be an outstanding creator of beauty.

Focusing on Relationship Beauty

When life is enriched with relationships, our opportunity for satisfaction grows.

Unlike the beauty of appearance, relationship beauty is something we can all attain.

Based on qualities respected across temporal, cultural, and religious divides, relationship beauty is free and accessible.

Refined, beauty is revealed by seven abilities. Together they form what I call *The Seven Strengths*. Flowing through personal and shared experience, their influence stands the test of time:

1. *Giving*

    Reflecting servanthood and sacrifice.

2. *Fortitude*

    Combining qualities of courage, perseverance, self-discipline, and patience.

3. *Honesty*

    Revealing willingness to be truthful in showing your real self.

4. *Heart*

    Embodying compassion, kindness, tolerance, and respect.

5. *Release*

    To enable forgiving, and learning to let go of hurt.

6. *Visioning*

    For seeing beyond the moment, through creative ideas, leadership, and inspiration.

7. *Wisdom*

    For discerning intentions, outcomes, and intelligently choosing.

Beauty Builds Meaning

Notably, *The Seven Strengths* will help you to find your own personal meaning of life and living.

Focusing on beauty in your relationships encourages you to reflect on your own unique qualities and the qualities you admire in others. By becoming more aware of your impact, you build your sense of personal purpose. The more purposeful, the more *complete* your life will feel.

Discerning and expressing what you know to be beautiful creates personal contentment. It also brings out the best in you.

Releasing the beauty of your vision holds the key to discovering the joy of a beautiful life.

Suggested Reading

Results from the Heart, Kiyoshi Suzaki, The Free Press, New York, 2002

42 Deep Thought on Life, the Universe, and Everything, Mark Vernon, A One World Book, Oxford, 2008.

The Creative Thinking Plan, Guy Claxton and Bill Lucas, Pearson Prentice Hall, London, 2007

Man's Search for Ultimate Meaning, Viktor Frankl, Plenum Press, New York, 1997

A New Earth: Awakening to Your Life's Purpose, Eckhardt Tolle, Michael Joseph an imprint of Penguin Books, New York, 2005

Get Up & Go Up, Tess Howells Schramm, A&J Printers, Tasmania, 1993

Rise, Ingrid Poulson, Pan McMillan Australia, 2008

What Color Is Your Parachute? 2009: A Practical Manual for Job-Hunters and Career-Changers, Richard Nelson-Bolles, Ten Speed Press, California, 2009

The Human Mind—And How to Make the Most of It, Robert Winston, Bantam Books, UK, 2004

Understanding People, Lawrence Crabb, Marshall Pickering (An Imprint of Harper Collins), New York, 1987

I Could Do Anything: If only I knew what it was, Barbara Sher with Barbara Smith, Hodder & Stoughton, Australia, 1998

Og Mandino's University of Success, Og Mandino, Bantam Books, USA & Canada, 1982

Women Who Think Too Much: How to break free of over-thinking and reclaim your life, Susan Nolen-Hoeksema, Henry Holt & Co, LLC, New York 2004

The Search for Meaning Collection, Caroline Jones, Dove (An Imprint of Harper Collins), Australia, 1995

The Compassionate Instinct: The Science of Human Goodness, edited by Dacher Keltner, Jason Marsh, and Jeremy Adam Smith, W.W. Norton & Co. Inc. New York, 2010

What's So Amazing about Grace? Philip Yancey, Strand Publishing, Sydney, 2000 (by special arrangement with Zondervan Publishing House, Grand Rapids, USA), 1997

The How of Happiness: A Practical Guide to Getting the Life You Want, Sonja Lyubomirsky, Sphere, London, 2007

Play, Stuart Brown, with Christopher Vaughan, Scribe, Melbourne, 2010

Business as Unusual, Anita Roddick, Thorsons, London, 2000

The 12 Secrets of Health & Happiness, Louise Samways, Penguin Books, Australia, 1997

Awaken the Giant Within, Anthony Robbins, Simon & Schuster, New York, 1992

The Secret Power of Beauty: Why happiness is in the eye of the beholder, John Armstrong, Penguin Books, London 2004

It's Not How Good You Are, It's How Good You Want to Be, Paul Arden, Phaidon, 2003

The Double Win, Dr. Denis Waitley, Berkley Books, New York, 1986

The Friendship Factor: How to get closer to the people you care for, Alan Loy McGinnis, Augsburg Publishing House, Minneapolis, 1979

Making Friends, Andrew Matthews, Media Masters, Singapore, 1992

The Way of the Wound: A Spirituality of Trauma and Transformation, Robert Grant, California USA, 1998

The Success Factor: Succeeding in Business & Life, Harry Stanton, William Collins, Australia, 1988

The Artist's Way at Work, Mark Bryan, Julia Cameron, & Catherine Allen, Pan Books, London, 1998

Coping with Grief, Mal McKissock & Dianne McKissock, ABC Books, Sydney, 2001

Psychology Today Magazine Last Reviewed 4 Jun 2007 Article ID: 3641, Jan/Feb 2005

The Philosophy of Beauty, Roger Cruden (BBC documentary on beauty in Art) screened in UK on BBC2 in 2010

49 Up, BBC Longitudinal Study on Children Growing Up in London in the 1960s

Life by Design, Dr. Rick Brinkman, Careertrack Publications, USA, 1992

Authentic Happiness: Using the New Positive Psychology to Realize Your Potential for Lasting Fulfillment, Martin Seligman, Press, New York, 2004

Happiness & Its Causes, Conference at Darling Harbor, Sydney, 2009

Index

acceptance 10-11, 14, 42, 94, 98, 126, 153, 158, 164, 172
activity 35, 53, 73, 115, 140, 145, 172
anger 20, 38, 61, 70, 137, 139, 157, 164, 174, 186
approval 42, 79, 91, 99-101, 110-111, 125, 134, 159, 196, 212
attractive 4, 12, 128, 133, 203, 210
belief 8, 11, 17, 77, 121, 140, 150, 158, 166, 181, 199
body 4, 8, 11, 13, 15, 23, 27-28
calm 5, 18, 33-36, 38, 47, 73, 92, 114, 117, 141, 143, 145, 161
change 27, 34, 48, 50, 87, 100, 115, 160, 165, 170, 177, 181
children 24, 49, 51, 69, 92, 98, 107, 134, 136, 157, 188-189, 191, 201-202
choice 9, 14, 40, 79, 80-82, 105, 161
communication 55, 97, 122
complexity 162
compromise 30, 188
confidence 10-11, 41, 71-72, 85, 88, 98, 118, 134, 139, 153, 158, 166, 180
confusion 54, 78, 124, 137, 199
consciousness 23, 121, 189
counseling 29, 123, 165

cruelty 59, 61, 63, 93, 94, 200
deception 32, 74, 196
denial 13, 71, 116, 156, 160, 162, 174, 206
depression 146-151, 183
determination 12, 150
dignity 39, 45, 49, 60-61, 114-115, 134, 141, 182-183, 187, 195
doubt 11, 70, 73, 79, 131, 142, 179
emotion 70, 74, 154, 161, 175-176, 187
faith 37, 78, 87
family 13-14, 17-18, 51, 69, 112, 124, 128, 145, 187-189, 190, 192-193, 197-200, 202
fears 111, 161, 165-169
food 26, 105, 170, 193
fortitude 46, 58, 64, 95, 151, 158, 169, 190, 198
friends 128-129, 146, 157, 161, 193, 212
giving 7, 17, 21, 32, 41, 44, 46, 53, 104, 110-111, 118-119, 133, 135, 158, 171, 183, 187
greed 59, 79, 163
grief 70, 171-175
habits 41-42, 118, 144, 146, 160, 173, 208
healing 9, 16, 95, 127, 144, 148, 158, 170, 176, 200
heart 46, 51, 109-110, 125, 128, 142-143, 171, 176, 190, 197, 202, 209

home 103, 126-129, 141, 143, 187, 191-194
honesty 7, 32, 54, 52, 56, 96, 116, 142, 165, 174, 192, 197-202
influence 15, 18, 25, 32-33, 38-40, 46, 57, 105, 113-115, 132, 142, 191
intimacy 17, 122-124, 152, 165, 203, 208-209
joy 67-69, 106, 127, 157, 181, 205
judging 105-106, 164
kindling 36-40
loneliness 110, 117, 157, 170-172
longings 111, 135, 203-204
love 11, 16-17, 69-71, 92, 95, 109-111, 116, 133, 153, 181, 183, 202-207
manipulation 91, 95-96, 186
meaning 8, 31, 66-71, 76-78, 81-82, 84-86, 88-89, 132, 135-136, 170, 180, 183
media 36, 51, 60, 74, 78, 188
money 10, 37, 50, 60, 132, 179-180, 182
pain 17, 56, 58-59, 109-111, 117, 152, 156-158, 170-171, 173, 184
patterns 21-22, 62, 69, 84, 97, 124, 159, 165, 178
play 50, 91-92, 105-16, 146, 190, 193
power 6-9, 16, 37, 39-40, 42, 76-78, 91, 94-96, 104
problems 29, 109, 110-111, 114, 117, 124, 185, 207
purpose 55, 67, 69-71, 76-79, 83-88, 120, 132-133, 183, 187, 203

reflection 21, 36
respect 10, 24-25, 28, 42, 49, 84, 100, 124, 142-143, 153
revering 20-21, 23-27, 95, 182
satisfaction 62, 67-68, 70, 79, 86-88, 119, 133, 135, 147, 157, 192
self-acceptance 10, 14, 98, 164
self-approval 100-101, 134, 1159, 196
self-awareness 84, 160
self-control 44-45, 157
self-doubt 10-11, 70, 73, 179
selfishness 33, 60, 62, 79, 96, 104, 115
sharing 39, 41-42, 62, 65, 122, 194, 208-209
silence 36, 141, 157, 174-175, 203
simplicity 41, 107
sleep 36, 89, 103, 143-144, 190-191
success 32, 137, 166, 186
tension 22, 107, 124, 178, 183
thinking 13, 18, 25-26, 31-38, 42-43, 84-85, 87-88, 98-99, 119-121, 142-144, 152-155, 160-161,
tolerance 143
trust 5-6, 11, 53, 55, 139, 185, 207
ugliness 06, 18, 25-26, 56-59, 61, 104-105, 119, 163, 182, 186
violence 44, 156, 200
visioning 46, 133, 195, 209
willpower 149-150, 171, 194
wisdom 44-47, 49, 52, 57-58, 104, 110-111, 113, 140, 159, 207

www.ingramcontent.com/pod-product-compliance
Lightning Source LLC
Chambersburg PA
CBHW070142100426
42743CB00013B/2799